THE COMPLETE UNRELIABLE MEMOIRS: VOLUME ONE

Clive James was the bestselling author of over forty books, including literary criticism, cultural essays, travel writing, verse and novels. He was the legendary TV critic of the *Observer* from 1972 to 1982. The hilarious and poignant *Unreliable Memoirs*, the first of five volumes of autobiography, has never been out of print since being published in 1980. He was a regular broadcaster on television and radio. His song-writing partnership with Pete Atkin spanned five decades. At the end of his life he returned to his first love, poetry. He published a translation of Dante's *Divine Comedy* and two critically acclaimed and bestselling collections of poems, *Sentenced to Life* and *Injury Time*, dealing with themes of illness, memory and regret. He was awarded the Philip Hodgins Memorial Medal for literature and a Special Award from the Orwell Prize for writing and broadcasting, and a lifetime achievement award from BAFTA. He died in 2019.

THE COMPLETE UNRELIABLE MEMOIRS: VOLUME ONE

Clive James

UNRELIABLE MEMOIRS
FALLING TOWARDS ENGLAND
MAY WEEK WAS IN JUNE

PICADOR
COLLECTION

This edition first published 2022 by Picador
an imprint of Pan Macmillan
The Smithson, 6 Briset Street, London EC1M 5NR
EU representative: Macmillan Publishers Ireland Ltd, 1st Floor,
The Liffey Trust Centre, 117–126 Sheriff Street Upper,
Dublin 1, D01 YC43
Associated companies throughout the world
www.panmacmillan.com

ISBN 978-1-5290-9076-5

Unreliable Memoirs first published 1980 by Jonathan Cape.
First published in paperback 1981 by Picador.
Falling Towards England first published 1985 by Jonathan Cape.
First published in paperback 1986 by Picador.
May Week Was In June first published 1990 by Jonathan Cape.
First published in paperback 1991 by Picador.

9 8 7 6 5 4 3 2 1

A CIP catalogue record for this book is available from the British Library.

Printed and bound by CPI Group (UK) Ltd, Croydon, CR0 4YY

UNRELIABLE MEMOIRS

To Rhoisin and Bruce Beresford

and the getting of wisdom

Andromache led the lamentation of the women, while she held in her hands the head of Hector, her great warrior:

.   'Husband, you are gone so young from life, and leave me in your home a widow. Our child is still but a little fellow, child of ill-fated parents, you and me. How can he grow up to manhood? Before that, this city shall be overthrown. For you are gone, you who kept watch over it, and kept safe its wives and their little ones . . .

'And you have left woe unutterable and mourning to your parents, Hector; but in my heart above all others bitter anguish shall abide. Your hands were not stretched out to me as you lay dying. You spoke to me no living word that I might have pondered as my tears fell night and day.'

Iliad, xxiv, translated by S. E. Winbolt,
from *The Iliad Pocket Book*, Constable 1911

Contents

Contents

Preface

Most first novels are disguised autobiographies. This autobiography is a disguised novel. On the periphery, names and attributes of real people have been changed and shuffled so as to render identification impossible. Nearer the centre, important characters have been run through the scrambler or else left out completely. So really the whole affair is a figment got up to sound like truth. All you can be sure of is one thing: careful as I have been to spare other people's feelings, I have been even more careful not to spare my own. Up, that is, of course, to a point.

Sick of being a prisoner of my childhood, I want to put it behind me. To do that, I have to remember what it was like. I hope I can dredge it all up again without sounding too pompous. Solemnity, I am well aware, is not my best vein. Yet it can't be denied that books like this are written to satisfy a confessional urge; that the mainspring of a confessional urge is guilt; and that somewhere underneath the guilt there must be a crime. In my case I suspect there are a thousand crimes, which until now I have mainly been successful in not recollecting. Rilke used to say that no poet would mind going to jail, since he would at least have time to explore the treasure house of his memory. In many respects Rilke was a prick.

Premature memoirs can only be conceited. I have no excuses against this charge, except to say that self-regard is itself a subject, and that to wait until reminiscence is justified by achievement might mean to wait for ever. I am also well aware that all attempts to put oneself in a bad light are doomed to be frustrated. The ego arranges the bad light to its own satisfaction. But on that point it is only necessary to remember Santayana's devastating comment on Rousseau's *Confessions*, which he said demonstrated, in equal measure, candour and ignorance of self. However adroitly I have calculated my intentional revelations, I can be sure that there are enough unintentional ones to give the reader an accurate impression. I had an absurdly carefree upbringing. If my account of it inspires disapproval, that can only serve to help redress the balance. One doesn't expect to get away with it for ever.

C.J.

1. THE KID FROM KOGARAH

I was born in 1939. The other big event of that year was the outbreak of the Second World War, but for the moment that did not affect me. Sydney in those days had all of its present attractions and few of the drawbacks. You can see it glittering in the background of the few photographs in which my father and I are together. Stocky was the word for me. Handsome was the word for him. Without firing a shot, the Japanese succeeded in extricating him from my clutches. Although a man of humble birth and restricted education, he was smart enough to see that there would be war in the Pacific. Believing that Australia should be ready, he joined up. That was how he came to be in Malaya at the crucial moment. He was at Parit Sulong bridge on the day when a lot of senior officers at last found out what their troops had guessed long before – that the Japanese army was better led and better equipped than anything we had to pit against it. After the battle my father walked all the way south to Singapore and arrived just in time for the surrender. If he had waited to be conscripted, he might have been sent to the Western Desert and spent a relatively happy few months fighting the kind of Germans whose essential decency was later to be portrayed on the screen by James Mason and Marlon Brando. As it was, he drew the short straw.

This isn't the place to tell the story of my mother and father – a story which was by no means over, even though they never saw one another again. I could get a lot of mileage out of describing how the good-looking young mechanic wooed and won the pretty girl who left school at fourteen and worked as an upholsterer at General Motors Holden. How the Depression kept them so poor

that they had to wait years to get married and have me. How fate
was cruel to both of them beyond measure. But it would be untrue
to them. It was thirty years or more before I even began to consider what my parents must have meant to each other. Before that
I hardly gave them a thought, except as vague occurrences on the
outskirts of a solipsistic universe. I can't remember my father at all.
I can remember my mother only through a child's eyes. I don't
know which fact is the sadder.

Anyway, my mother let our little house in Kogarah and we
went to stay with my Aunt Dot in Jannali, another half hour
down the Illawarra line. This move was made on the advice of my
father, who assumed that the centre of Sydney would be flattened
by Japanese bombs about two hours after the whistle blew. The
assumption proved to be ill-founded, but the side effects were
beneficial, since Jannali was a perfect spot to grow up in. There
were only a dozen or so streets in the whole area. Only one of them
was paved. The railway line ran through a cutting somewhere in
the middle. Everything else was bush.

The houses were made of either weatherboard or fibro. Ours
was weatherboard. Like all the others, it was surrounded by an area
of land which could be distinguished from the bush only because
of its even more lavish concentrations of colour. Nasturtiums and
honeysuckle proliferated, their strident perfumes locked in perpetual contention. Hydrangeas grew in reefs, like coral in a sea of
warm air. At the bottom of the backyard lay an air-raid trench full
of rainwater. I fell into it within minutes of arriving. Hearing a
distant splash, Aunt Dot, who was no sylph, came through the
back door like a train out of a tunnel and hit the lawn running.
The door, a fly-screen frame with a return spring, made exactly the
same sound as one of those punching-bags you try your strength
on. Aunt Dot was attired in a pink corset but it didn't slow her
down. She covered the ground like Marjorie Jackson, the girl who
later became famous as the Lithgow Flash. The earth shook. I was
going down for the third time but I can distinctly remember the
moment she launched herself into the air, describing a parabolic

trajectory which involved, at one point, a total eclipse of the sun. She landed in the trench beside me. Suddenly we were sitting together in the mud. All the water was outside on the lawn.

Usually my mother was first to the rescue. This time she was second. She had to resuscitate both of us. She must have been in the front of the house looking after my grandfather. He needed a lot of looking after. Later on my mother told me that he had always been a selfish man. She and Aunt Dot had given a good part of their lives to waiting on him. Mentally, he had never left England. I remember him as a tall, barely articulate source of smells. The principal smells were of mouldy cloth, mothballs, seaweed, powerful tobacco and the tars that collect in the stem of a very old pipe. When he was smoking he was invisible. When he wasn't smoking he was merely hard to pick out in the gloom. You could track him down by listening for his constant, low-pitched, incoherent mumble. From his carpet slippers to his moustache was twice as high as I could reach. The moustache was saffron with nicotine. Everywhere else he was either grey or tortoiseshell mottle. His teeth were both.

I remember he bared them at me one Christmas dinner. It was because he was choking on a coin in a mouthful of plum pudding. It was the usual Australian Christmas dinner, taking place in the middle of the day. Despite the temperature being 100°F. in the shade, there had been the full panoply of ragingly hot food, topped off with a volcanic plum pudding smothered in scalding custard. My mother had naturally spiced the pudding with sixpences and threepenny bits, called zacs and trays respectively. Grandpa had collected one of these in the oesophagus. He gave a protracted, strangled gurgle which for a long time we all took to be the beginning of some anecdote. Then Aunt Dot bounded out of her chair and hit him in the back. By some miracle she did not snap his calcified spine. Coated with black crumbs and custard, the zac streaked out of his mouth like a dumdum and ricocheted off a tureen.

Grandpa used to take me on his knee and read me stories, of

which I could understand scarcely a word, not because the stories were over my head but because his speech by that stage consisted entirely of impediments. 'Once upon a mpf,' he would intone, 'there wah ngung mawg blf...' My mother got angry with me if I was not suitably grateful to Grandpa for telling me stories. I was supposed to dance up and down at the very prospect. To dodge this obligation, I would build cubbyholes. Collecting chairs, cushions, bread-boards and blankets from all over the house, I would assemble them into a pillbox and crawl in, plugging the hole behind me. Safe inside, I could fart discreetly while staring through various eye-slits to keep track of what was going on. From the outside I was just a pair of marsupial eyeballs in a heap of household junk, topped off with a rising pall of sulphuretted hydrogen. It was widely conjectured that I was hiding from ghosts. I was, too, but not as hard as I was hiding from Grandpa. When he shuffled off to bed, I would unplug my igloo and emerge. Since my own bedtime was not long after dark, I suppose he must have been going to bed in the late afternoon. Finally he went to bed altogether.

With Grandpa laid up, I was the man of the house, except when Uncle Vic or Ray came home on leave. Uncle Vic was Aunt Dot's husband and Ray was her son, therefore my cousin. Uncle Vic was an infantry corporal stationed in New Guinea. Sometimes when he got leave he would bring his Owen gun home, minus the bolt. I was allowed to play with the gun. It was huge. I stumbled around pointing it at bull-ants' nests. The bull-ants, however, didn't bluff so easily. The only argument they understood was a few gallons of boiling water poured down their central stairwell. I once saw Uncle Vic administer this treatment, in revenge after half a dozen bull-ants stung me on the right foot. They were the big red kind with the black bag at the back. When that size bull-ant stings you, you stay stung. My foot came up like a loaf of bread. I just lay in the road and screamed. The same foot got into even worse trouble later on, as I shall relate.

While I staggered around blasting the nasturtiums, Uncle Vic did a lot of enigmatic smiling. One day I struggled all the way down to the railway cutting so that I could show the gun to some local children I hoped to impress. They hadn't waited. I could see them climbing the hill on the other side of the railway line. I shouted to them, holding the gun up as high as I could, which I suppose was no height at all. They couldn't hear me. I think it was the first big disappointment of my life. When I came back dragging the gun through the dirt, Uncle Vic did a bit more of his enigmatic smiling. Talking to him years later, I realized why he was so quiet at the time. It was because he wasn't too thrilled about what he had seen in New Guinea. Japanese scouts used to sneak up on our sentries through the thick white morning jungle mist and punch meat-skewers through their heads from ear to ear.

Ray was more forthcoming, until he got sick. He was a fitter with the RAAF somewhere up there but after his first leave he never went back. He just stayed around the house in his dressing gown, getting thinner. He used to let me stand on his feet while he walked me around. The game was called Giant Steps. I loved it. Then the day came when he didn't want to play it any more. My mother told me he wasn't strong enough. I got into trouble at the dinner table when I asked him why he was holding his fork with both hands.

So really my mother was the only pillar of strength available. One parent is enough to spoil you but discipline takes two. I got too much of what I wanted and not enough of what I needed. I was a child who was picked up. The effects have stayed with me to this day, although in the last few years I have gradually learned to blame myself instead of circumstances. My mother had a strong will but she would have had to be Fabius Cunctator to cope with my tantrums when I didn't feel like going to school. Every second day I played sick and stayed home. Her only alternative was to see how far she could drag me. She would have had a better chance dragging a dead horse through soft sand. The school was a single-room wooden hut with twelve desks. Painted cream, it sat in half an acre of dirt playground about a mile from our house. Bushfires burned it down every couple of years but unfortunately it was easy to replace. The first year of school wasn't so bad. I liked Miss Dear. Usually I got more questions right than anybody else and was awarded first choice of blocks. I chose the set with the arches and the columns. I would go off on my own into a corner of the playground and build structures akin to the Alhambra or the Escorial, throwing a fit if any other child tried to interfere.

Even the best set of school blocks wasn't as good as the set I had at home. Passed on to me by Grandpa, they were satin-smooth Victorian creations of inch-by-inch oak, every length from one to twelve inches, plus arches, Doric columns, metopes, triglyphs and sundry other bits and pieces. With them I could build a tower much taller than myself. The usual site was the middle of the lounge room. A length of cotton could be tied to one of the lower columns, so that I could retire into hiding and collapse the tower by remote control at the precise moment when Aunt Dot lumbered into range. It made a noise like Valhalla falling. She would have one of her turns – these needed plenty of space – and demand that I be sent to school next day.

Toys were scarce. A few crude lead soldiers were still produced so that children could go on poisoning themselves but otherwise there was almost nothing. It was a big event when my mother bought me a little painted red cow. Presumably it was English. I took it to school and lost it. Next day she came with me to school, wanting to find out what had happened to it. My carelessness with everything she bought me went on hurting her for years. She construed it, accurately, as ingratitude. From the sensitivity angle I was about as obtuse as a child can be. I was sensitive enough about myself, but that's a different thing.

School, passable for the first year, became unbearable in the second, when the kind Miss Dear was supplanted by a hard case called Miss Turnbull. Dark, cold and impatient, Miss Turnbull might have been the firm hand I needed, but already I was unable to cope with authority. I still can't today, tending to oscillate between nervous flippancy and overly solicitous respect. In those days, when I was about a third of my present height and a quarter of the weight, there was nothing to do except duck. I did everything to get out of facing up to Miss Turnbull. I had Mondayitis every day of the week. As my mother dragged me down the front path, I would clutch my stomach, cross my eyes, stick out my tongue, cough, choke, scream and vomit simultaneously.

But there were some occasions when I ended up at school no matter what I did. It was then revealed that I had Dropped Behind the Class. Words I could not recognize would come up on the spelling wheel. The spelling wheel was a thick card with a window in it and a cardboard disc behind. As you turned the disc, words appeared one at a time in the window. I remember not being able to pronounce the word 'the'. I pronounced it 'ter-*her*'. The class had collective hysterics. They were rolling around on the floor with their knees up. I suppose one of the reasons why I grew up feeling the need to cause laughter was perpetual fear of being its unwitting object.

From the start of Miss Turnbull's reign until the day we left Jannali, every morning I would shout the house down. For my mother, the path leading from the front porch to the front gate became a Via Dolorosa. My act reached ever new heights of extravagance. Either it worked or it didn't. If it didn't I would sit in school praying for the bushfires to come early and incinerate the place. If it did I would either hang around the house or go and play with Ron, a truant of my own age who lived next to Hally the butcher down near the station. Ron was a grub. I was always being warned off him because he was so filthy. He and I used to squat under his house tweaking each other's ding, watching each other pee, and so on. I can't remember it all now. I suppose I have repressed it. If there was any sexual excitement, it took the form of intense curiosity, just as I was curious about my mother when we were in the bath together. I remember the shock of seeing Ray undressed. He looked as if he had a squirrel hanging there. I had an acorn.

Ron's wreck of a mother used to give us buttered bread with

hundreds and thousands on it. It was like being handed a slice of powdered rainbow. They must have been a poor family but I remember my visits to them as luxuries. As well as the Technicolor bread and butter, there were vivid, viscid green drinks made from some kind of cordial. Ron's place would have been Beulah Land except for one drawback. They had a cattle dog called Bluey. A known psychopath, Bluey would attack himself if nothing else was available. He used to chase himself in circles trying to bite his own balls off. To avert instant death, I was supposed to call out from the front gate when I arrived and not open it until I was told that Bluey had been chained up. One day I opened it too early and Bluey met me on the front path. I don't know where he had come from – probably around the side of the house – but it was as if he had come up out of the ground on a lift. He was nasty enough when chained up but on the loose he was a bad dream. Barking from the stomach, he opened a mouth like a great, wet tropical flower. When he snapped it shut, my right foot was inside it.

If Bluey hadn't been as old as the hills, my foot would have come right off. Luckily his teeth were in ruins, but even so I was only a few tendons short of becoming an amputee. Since Bluey's spittle obviously contained every bacterium known to science, my frantic mother concluded that the local doctor would not be enough. I think I went to some kind of hospital in Sutherland. Needles were stuck into me while she had yet another case of heart failure. Bluey was taken away to be destroyed. Looking back on it, I can see that this was tough on Bluey, who had grown old in the belief that biting ankles was the thing to do. At the time I was traumatized. I loathed dogs from that day forward. They could sense my terror from miles away. Any dog could back me against a wall for hours. Eventually I learned not to show fear. The breakthrough came when I managed to walk away from a dog who had me bailed up against the door of a garage. Admittedly he was only a Pekinese about eight inches long, but it was still a triumph. That was more than a year ago.

2. VALLEY OF THE KILLER SNAKES

Such incidents must have been hell on my mother's nerves. I would have been enough of a handful even in normal circumstances but the sweat of looking after me was made worse by her uncertainty about what was happening to my father. She got some news of him when he was in Changi but after he was moved to Japan there was not much to go on. The mail from Kobe, when there was any, was so censored it looked like shredded lettuce. During the last part of the war she wasn't even certain that he was alive. In those circumstances it couldn't have been much help to her, having the kind of son who goes off and gets half-eaten by a dog.

Lesser catastrophes were no doubt just as wearing, since they happened all the time. My collection of marbles consisted mainly of priceless connie agates handed down by Grandpa. Ocean crystals, iced roses and butterflies in amber, they tumbled from their draw-string bag like a Byzantine avalanche. I took them out and lost the lot to a local thug called Mick Roach. Years older than I, Mick dated up clay-dabs against my connies. A clay-dab, as its name suggests, could be dissolved in water or squeezed flat with a thumb. Mick used steelies for taws. Steelies were ball bearings an inch in diameter. They blasted my defenceless cannon-fodder from the ring. On top of his superior artillery, Mick could actually play marbles, whereas I had no idea of what I was doing, otherwise I would not have allowed him to readjust the size of the ring for each go. When it was his turn, the ring was about four inches in diameter. When it was my turn, the Arunta tribe could have held a corroboree around its circumference.

I lurched home in tears, trailing an empty bag. My mother went berserk. She tried to shame Mick's parents into giving my marbles back, but Mick's father talked some confident nonsense about a fair fight. 'If your father was here,' said my mother with a strangely shaking voice, 'there'd be a fair fight.' I wish I could say that I shared her anger, but I think I was just embarrassed about the fuss. I wanted my mistakes forgotten, not faced up to – the foundations of a bad habit.

Quite apart from moral disasters, there was the question of my physical safety. Even after Bluey's demise, there was still good reason to believe that I would do myself an injury if left unsupervised. I had a terrifying gift for carving myself up. Running around barefoot, I would go out of my way to jump on a broken bottle. Gashes caused by rusty corrugated iron were treated with Acriflavine, an antiseptic that turned the surrounding skin variously blue and yellow, so that I looked half ancient Briton, half Inca. The only asphalt road in the area led down to the railway line at about the same angle as a door-wedge. It might not sound a very perilous incline, but I was able to prove empirically that it was more than steep enough for a small boy on a tricycle to attain terminal velocity. The pedals became a vicious blur. There was no hope of getting my feet back on them. It was apparent that I would arrive at the bottom of the hill just in time to be flung onto the line in the path of a train even then looming out of the cutting. Hearing my screams, my mother came after me like the back half of Zeno's paradox about Achilles and the tortoise, if you can imagine Achilles in drag and the tortoise screaming its head off while balanced on a shaking bicycle seat with its legs stuck out. She caught up with me at the last moment. It was part of the pattern. I always survived, but only after scaring her to death.

And then there were Australia's natural wonders. Jannali was not quite the bush proper, but it was certainly an outer suburb. You could walk over the next hill and be back in the sort of country that the convicts used to die in when they ran away. Not that they would necessarily have died of hunger. There is plenty for you to eat. Unfortunately there is also plenty that wants to eat you.

By now I have grown used to the benevolence of the English countryside, where there are no natural hazards beyond the odd clump of poison ivy, a few varieties of inimical mushroom and half a dozen adders all of which wear number plates and have exclusive contracts with BBC television. Walking at ease in such an Augustan context, it is sometimes difficult to remember what it was like to inhabit a land crawling with danger. I have already mentioned the bull-ants. There were also snakes. Walking to school bare-footed along dirt paths lined with banksias and waratahs, I was always expecting to meet one of the snakes portrayed in the gaudily detailed charts which were hung up in the railway station and the post office. Luckily the only snakes I ever encountered were harmless civilians: the filing clerks and secretaries of the serpentine world. But Uncle Vic caught a full-sized fighting snake right outside our front gate. It was a black snake – one step worse than a brown snake. A black snake can kill an adult if it is big enough. This one was big enough. Uncle Vic pinned it to the ground in the middle but both ends of it went on trying to get at him.

The next step up from the black snake is the tiger snake. It was statistically likely that at least a few tiger snakes were in our district, probably holed up in some shack and sending their girlfriends out to buy liquor. Over and above the tiger snake, so to speak, is the taipan. Luckily ours was not taipan country. Indeed at that time the taipan was not yet famous anywhere. Up in Queensland, in the sugar-cane belt, the taipan was soon to begin making headlines and getting its photograph in *Pix*. Tiger snakes and black snakes can't compete with taipans, but they are bad enough. Brown snakes are pretty bad. Allegedly harmless snakes don't look very benevolent either. I used to think about all this a lot on the way to or from school. Whether to run fast or tiptoe silently was a constant dilemma, which I tried to solve by doing both at once.

I also thought about spiders. Two of the worst Australian spiders are the funnel-web and the trap-door. One is even more lethal than the other but I can't remember which. It doesn't matter, because either can put a child in peril of its life. The funnel-web is

a ping-pong ball in a fox-fur. It inhabits a miniature missile silo in
the ground, from which it emerges in a savage arc, ready to sink
its mandibles into anything that breathes. The trap-door spider is
really a funnel-web plus cunning, since it conceals the mouth of
its silo with a tiny coal-hole door. Both kinds of spider can leap
an incredible distance. A woodpile might contain hundreds of each
kind. If you even suspected the presence of either species in your
garden you were supposed to report immediately to the responsible authorities. After the war an English immigrant lady became
famous when she was discovered gaily swatting funnel-webs with a
broom as they came flying at her in squadrons. Any one of them,
if it had got close enough even to spit at her, would have put her
in bed for a year.

   I somehow managed to avoid meeting trap-door spiders or
funnel-webs. Quite often I came face to face with a harmless
relative, which Aunt Dot called a tarantula and I called a triantelope. Actually it was just a common garden spider called the
huntsman, whose idea of a big thrill was to suck a wasp. The
huntsman wove big vertical webs which I used regularly to walk
into when heading tentatively down the back path to the lavatory
after dark. Getting mixed up in the web, to which I knew the
triantelope must be at some point attached, was a frightening
sensation which I attempted to forestall by inching forward very
slowly, with one hand held out. It didn't help.

   But the real horror among spiders was more likely to be
encountered in the lavatory itself. This was the red-back. The
red-back is mainly black, with a scarlet stripe down where its
spine would be if it were a vertebrate. Looking like a neatly rigged
and painted single-seater that might once have been flown by von
Richthofen, the red-back had enough poison in it to immobilize a
horse. It had the awkward habit, in unsewered areas like ours, of
lurking under the lavatory seat. If a red-back bit you on the behind
you were left with the problem of where to put the tourniquet and
not long to think about it. Nor could you ask anyone to suck out

the poison, unless you knew them very well indeed. I saw plenty of red-backs and actually got bitten by one, luckily not on the behind. I think it was a red-back. Certainly I told my mother it was. Once again the site of the wound was my right foot, which by this time must have been looking as if it belonged to Philoctetes. My mother knelt, sucked and spat. We were both frightened but she was not too frightened to act. She must have been getting tired, however, of being both father and mother.

After the first atomic bomb there was a general feeling that Japan had surrendered. The street was decorated with bunting. Strings of all the Allied flags were hung up between the flame trees. The Japanese missed their cue and all the bunting had to be taken in. Finally the Japanese saw the point and all the bunting was taken out again. Everybody was in ecstasies except my mother, who still had no news. Then an official telegram came to say that he was all right. Letters from my father arrived. They were in touch with each other and must have been very happy. The Americans, with typical generosity, arranged that all the Australian POWs in Japan should be flown home instead of having to wait for ships. My mother started counting the days. Then a telegram arrived saying that my father's plane had been caught in a typhoon and had crashed in Manila Bay with the loss of everyone aboard.

Up until that day, all the grief and worry that I had ever seen my mother give way to had been tempered for my ears. But now she could not help herself. At the age of five I was seeing the full force of human despair. There were no sedatives to be had. It was several days before she could control herself. I understood nothing beyond the fact that I could not help. I think that I was marked for life. I know now that until very recent years I was never quite all there – that I was play-acting instead of living and that nothing except my own unrelenting fever of self-consciousness seemed quite real. Eventually, in my middle thirties, I got a grip on myself. But there can be no doubt that I had a tiresomely protracted adolescence, wasting a lot of other people's time, patience and love.

I suppose it is just another sign of weakness to blame everything
on that one moment, but it would be equally dishonest if I failed
to record its piercing vividness.

As for my mother, I don't presume even to guess at what she
felt. The best I can say is that at least they got the chance of writing
a few words to one another before the end. In one respect they
were like Osip and Nadezhda Mandelstam in the last chapters of
Hope against Hope – torn apart in mid-word without even the
chance to say goodbye. But in another way they were not. My
father had taken up arms out of his own free will. In Europe,
millions of women and children had been killed for no better
reason than some ideological fantasy. My father was a free human
being. So was my mother. What happened to them, terrible though
it was, belongs in the category of what Nadezhda Mandelstam,
elsewhere in that same great book, calls the privilege of ordinary
heartbreaks. Slowly, in those years, the world was becoming aware
that things had been happening which threw the whole value of
human existence into doubt. But my father's death was not one
of them. It was just bad luck. I have disliked luck ever since –
an aversion only increased by the fact that I have always been
inordinately lucky.

Grandpa's death was easier for me to deal with. Everybody
was ready for it. Grief was kept in bounds. There was no way
of pinpointing the moment when he passed to the beyond. In his
dark bedroom he merely turned into a slightly more immobile
version of what he had already been for years. It was time to open
the windows and let in the light. I was encouraged to take a look
at the corpse – a wise decision, since it immediately became clear
to me that there are more terrible things than dying a natural
death. The old man merely looked as if he had been bored out of
existence. Perhaps I got it all wrong then and have still got it all
wrong now. Perhaps he died in a redemptive ecstasy after being
vouchsafed a revelation of the ineffable. But I doubt it. I think he
just croaked.

Ray was harder to be blasé about. We hadn't played Giant Steps for a long time. Eventually he was too weak to stand. He was taken away to the military hospital at Yaralla, where over the next few years he gradually wasted to nothing. He used to smile at me through the mirror mounted over his face as he lay in the iron lung. The smile took an age to arrive and another age to go away. It was like watching sand dry in the sun. I can remember being scolded for not caring enough. I think it was Aunt Dot who did the scolding. The unremitting gradualness of it all must have been hard for her to take. People's emotions are no less real just because they carry on a lot. Aunt Dot could do the mad scene from *Lucia* when her lemon-meringue pie collapsed. But there is no reason to believe that she felt her bereavement any the less for feeling little things too much. She was, and is, a good woman who would have mothered me if she had been called upon. Mothering, however, wasn't what I was short of.

My mother decided it was time to go back to our house at No. 6 Margaret Street, Kogarah, a place I couldn't remember having seen. There was nothing to keep us in Jannali, where losses appeared to be accumulating steadily. Changing schools was certainly no great wrench. There were no playmates I would particularly miss, except perhaps the unspeakable Ron. I was taken to a party that year where there was a present for every child except me. It turned out that my present, a box of soldiers, had been mislaid. The mistake was quickly rectified. But it took all afternoon and half the night to coax me down from my tree. Definitely time for a change of scene.

Besides, Kogarah was more of a built-up area, and therefore, my mother reasoned, safer. It would even have the sewer on soon – an unheard-of luxury. The only problem was to get the tenants out. They had promised to move when asked, but by now there was a housing shortage and they didn't want to go. My mother, however, had lost too much. She wouldn't stand for losing her house as well. It had cost her and my father everything they had ever earned. She was firm about not letting the tenants break their agreement. Out they went and in we moved.

Even in my memory the house is small. Early on there were a lounge, two bedrooms, a kitchen-dining room, a bathroom and a back veranda, with laundry and lavatory built into the back wall. Later we had the back veranda enclosed with fibro and Cooper louvres so that it could count as a room too. Between the front fence and the paved street there was a concrete footpath and a piece of lawn, known as the front strip, which included a box-gum tree big enough for a child to swing upside down from and drop on its head. Every household mowed its own front strip. It was to be a constant source of shame to my mother that our piece of front strip was never as finely mown or sharply edged as the front strips of the next-door neighbours.

From the front fence to the house was the front lawn. There was a car's width of lawn down the right side of the house, leading in almost every case but ours to a garage. This was called the driveway whether you had a car or not. On the other side of the house was a much narrower passage between house and fence, just wide enough to walk through. Behind the house was a backyard. Most of this, in our case, was lawn: a mixture of buffalo grass, couch and tenacious crops of paspalum. There were passion-fruit vines growing on the fence where the garage should have been. In the opposite back corner was a peach tree, in which over the years I made various attempts, all unsuccessful, to build a tree house. There were patches of vegetable garden along all three edges of the backyard. These were devoted to the growing of the kind of vegetables I always refused to eat – chocos, beetroot, rhubarb and so on. Or is rhubarb a fruit? Despite my mother's imprecations, I could never see the point of the choco. Whatever you do with it, it's still nothing. It looks like an albino avocado and tastes like cellophane. Its only advantage lies in its cheapness. You can't stop chocos growing. It takes a flamethrower to keep them down.

The widest of these vegetable patches lay parallel to the back fence, beyond which was a poultry farm inhabited by thousands of chooks all synchronized to wake you up at dawn. Later on the farm became a housing estate. Whatever lay beyond the back fence,

I was always tunnelling towards it. The back patch was the site of my unflagging efforts to get back to the womb by digging into the earth. I started this at quite an early age, attaining more proficiency as time went on. My early burrows were simple dugouts roofed over with box tops, after which the earth was heaped back on. There was just room for me. I would persuade my mother to cover up the entrance and leave me down there all afternoon. It didn't matter if the thing collapsed – it was only a few inches of dirt. Older children had been known to try the same trick in sand dunes, with fatal results. She probably reasoned that it was better to let me indulge these fantasies where she could keep an eye on me.

Over the next few years, the back patch started looking like the Ypres Salient. I would dig complicated networks of trenches, roof them over, and continued tunnelling from inside, honeycombing the clay all the way down to the water table. Other boys in the street were fascinated. It became known that I was taking my Donald Duck comics down there and reading them by torchlight. They, too, turned up with armfuls of comics. Suddenly I had friends. I had stumbled on one of the secrets of leadership – start something, then let people know you are doing them a favour by bringing them in on it. Candidates for my tunnel club had to go through a probationary period of hovering on the outskirts. It was like being put up for the Garrick. Finally half the small boys in the district were spending the whole weekend somewhere under our backyard. Similar scenes must have occurred on the night of the Great Escape from Stalag Luft III. I overdid it when I started letting the little kids down there. Little kids, I should have known, ruin things. Geoffrey Teichmann was only about four years old. Crawling somewhere down around Level 7 leading off Shaft 4, he brushed against one of the fruit-case slats I used for pit-props. The whole system fell on him. Parents arrived from everywhere to dig the little twerp out. That was the end of that.

But my new-found acceptability was strictly a local phenomenon. School was still a nightmare. I went to Kogarah Infants'

School and then to Kogarah Primary. They were both in the same place, near Kogarah station, more than a mile away on the trolleybus. The fare was a penny. The trolleybus went down Rocky Point Road, through a shopping centre called the Bundy, then turned left to cut across Prince's Highway and climb over the hill to the station, where it either turned around at the Loop or went on to Rockdale. There were shops at the Loop, including Parry's Milk Bar, the centre of local nightlife for years to come. Being bought a fruit sundae in Parry's late at night was pretty well the most luxurious thing that could happen to you.

Two minutes' walk up the hill from the Loop was the school. I could make that two minutes last an hour – sometimes a whole day. If it had not been for another boy called McGowan, I would have been cast as the school's problem child. Luckily McGowan was so disturbed that I seemed unobtrusive by comparison. A ginger shambles, McGowan wore glasses with one lens covered up by brown sticky paper, presumably to correct a fault of vision. He screamed without provocation, frothed at the mouth, bit pieces out of other children and kicked teachers in the stomach. In the playground he would run at the supervising teacher while her back was turned, so that he would be going at full speed when she wheeled at the sound of his running footsteps. He was thus able to get plenty of force behind the kick. The teacher would be taken away on a stretcher. Eventually there were no longer any members of the staff willing to take on the job of supervising any classroom or playground with McGowan in it, so he was removed. That left me looking more conspicuous.

The only thing I liked about school was skipping around in circles until the music stopped, then lying down on the floor for Quiet Time. I was very good at Quiet Time. Otherwise it was all a bit hopeless. I piddled on the floor when it was my turn to sing. Conversely, I got caught drinking my daily bottle of milk in the lavatory. For some reason this was regarded as a fearful crime. My mother used to pick me up after school. One day we missed each other and I went home alone on the bus. Meanwhile my mother was going frantic at the school. There were mutual tears that night. Next day when I answered my name at the morning assembly roll-call, the headmistress said, 'Ah yes, that's the little boy who ran away from his mother.' Thanks a lot, witch. I kacked my pants on the spot.

The whole secret of kacking your pants, incidentally, is to produce a rock-solid blob which will slide down your leg in one piece and can be rolled away into hiding at the point of the toe. That way, your moment of shame can be kept to the proportions of a strictly local disaster. But if you let go with anything soft, it takes two teachers to clean you up and the whole affair attracts nationwide publicity. You get people interviewing you.

3. BILLYCART HILL

The name I answered to in my early years was Vivian James. Later on my mother gave me my choice of new first names and I picked Clive out of a Tyrone Power movie. She sympathized with the fix she and my father had got me into by naming me after Vivian McGrath, star of the 1938 Davis Cup squad. After Vivien Leigh played Scarlett O'Hara the name became irrevocably a girl's name no matter how you spelled it, so those few little boys who had been saddled with it went through hell. I just got sick of ending up on the wrong lists, being sent to sewing classes, etc. Children in Australia are still named after movies and sporting events. You can tell roughly the year the swimming star Shane Gould was born. It was about the time *Shane* was released. There was a famous case of a returned serviceman who named his son after all the campaigns he had been through in the Western Desert. The kid was called William Bardia Escarpment Qattara Depression Mersa Matruh Tobruk El Alamein Benghazi Tripoli Harris.

Things marginally improved when I was promoted, a year early, from the Infants' School to the Primary School. The embarrassments of co-education were at last left behind. No longer were we obliged to pair off and hold hands tweely when marching into the classroom – a huge advance on previous conditions. I achieved early promotion solely through being good at reading. The reason I was good at reading had nothing to do with school. In our last year at Jannali I had started to pick my way through Grandpa's musty old bound sets of *Wide World* magazine. Also there were bright yellow heaps of the *National Geographic*. In our first years at Kogarah, while searching my mother's room, I found the wardrobe half full of magazines. These were mainly *Picture Post, Lilli-put, Collier's,* the *Saturday Evening Post, Life* and *Reader's Digest.* I started off by looking at the pictures but gradually progressed to being able to read the text.

I can't remember what it was like not to be able to read English fluently. Nowadays, if I am learning to read a new language, I try to savour the moment that separates not knowing how to from not knowing how not to. At the time, I simply found myself able to read. Over the next few years I absorbed everything in those few hundred magazines. I read them until there was nothing left to read and then read them again until the covers pulled away from the staples. The *Saturday Evening Post*s with the Norman Rockwell covers satisfied every demand of my aesthetic sense, the gustatory requirements included. I used to read them instead of eating. I felt about them the way Turgenev felt about the emblem book he wrote of to Bakunin, and made a part of Laretsky's childhood in *A Nest of Gentlefolk.*

I suppose if I had been John Stuart Mill I would have sought out a better class of reading matter. Indeed my father and mother had done a lot of fairly solid reading together: stacked away at the top of the cupboard in the hall were cheap sets of Dickens, Thackeray and the Brontës. For some reason I was never to seek them out, even in my teens. I always had an automatic aversion to the set books. Reading off the course was in my nature. My style was to read everything except what mattered, just as I ate everything except what was good for me.

In primary school I ceased being the class half-wit and became class smart-alec instead. This presented a whole new set of difficulties. Coming out first in the term tests attracted accusations of being teacher's pet. It was true, alas: Mr Slavin, although a fair-minded man, couldn't help smiling upon anyone who knew how to answer the questions. Too many boys in the class had trouble remembering their own names. Most of the heat was focused on an unfortunate called Thommo, who was caned regularly. For ordinary offences Thommo was caned by Mr Slavin and for more serious transgressions he was caned by the deputy headmaster. Mr Slavin was authorized to impart up to four strokes. Thommo usually required six even to slow him down. We used to sit silent while the deputy head gave Thommo the treatment outside in the corridor. The six strokes took some time to deliver, because Thommo had to be recaptured after each stroke, and to be recaptured he had first to be found. His screams and sobs usually gave away his location, but not always. One day the police came to the classroom and made Thommo open his Globite school case. It was full of stolen treasures from Coles and Woolworths: balloons, bulldog paper clips, funny hats, a cut-glass vase. Thommo was led howling away and never seen again.

Despite Thommo's fate, on the whole I would rather have been him than me. His manly activities merited respect. As teacher's pet, I was regarded with envy, suspicion and hatred. I had not yet learned to joke my way out of trouble and into favour. Instead I tried to prove that I, too, could be rebellious, untrammelled, dangerous and tough. To register, any demonstration of these qualities would have to be made in view of the whole class. This would not be easy, since my desk was at the back of the room. There were five columns of desks with seven desks in each column. The five most academically able boys sat in the back five desks and so on down the line, with the desks at the front containing the dullards, psychopaths, Thommo, etc. The problem was to become the cynosure of all eyes in some way more acceptable than my usual method of throwing my hand in the air, crying 'Sir! Sir! Sir!', and supplying the correct answer.

The solution lay in the network of railways tracks carved into the top of each desk by successive generations of occupants. Along these tracks fragments of pencil, pen holders or bits of chalk could be pushed with chuffing noises. I also found out that the exposed wood was susceptible to friction. At home I was already an established fire-bug, running around with a magnifying glass frying sugar-ants. I had learned something of what pieces of wood could do to each other. This knowledge I now applied, rubbing the end of my box-wood ruler against the edge of one of the tracks. A wisp of smoke came up. Eyes turned towards me. The wisp became a billow. More eyes turned towards me. The billow was fretted with fire. Mr Slavin's eyes turned towards me.

He gave me his full four strokes. The pain was considerable, but the glory was greater. 'What's sauce for the goose,' he said as I tucked my smarting hands under my armpits, 'is sauce for the gander.' Mr Slavin's epigrams were distinctly sub-Wildean but he had a knack for trotting them out at precisely the appropriate moment. He might even have had an inkling of how much I wanted to be a goose.

This small triumph spurred me fatally towards bigger things. There was a craze on for dongers. Crazes came one after the other. There was a craze for a game of marbles called followings. There was a craze for cigarette cards: not the cards that used to come in packets of English cigarettes, but cards made elaborately out of the cigarette packets themselves. The cards had different values according to brands, with English Gold Flake scoring highest and Australian Craven 'A' scoring lowest. You flicked your cards at a wall. The one who finished nearest the wall got a chance to toss all the cards in the air at once. The ones that fell face up were his. Bottletops worked roughly the same way, except that the one who got closest to the wall stacked all the bottletops on his upturned elbow and then swiped downwards with his hand, getting to keep as many of the bottletops as he could catch between hand and wrist. It is difficult to describe and even more difficult to do. I always lost. I wasn't bad at cock-a-lorum, but falling over on the asphalt playground added painfully to my usual array of sores and scabs. The craze I hoped to be good at was dongers.

A donger was an ordinary handkerchief folded into a triangle. You held each end of the hypotenuse and twirled until the handkerchief had rolled itself tight. Then you held the two ends together in one hand while you rolled the fat centre part even tighter with the other. The result was then soaked in water to give it weight. The more reckless boys sometimes inserted a lead washer or a small rock. The completed donger was, in effect, a blackjack. Every playtime, with me hovering cravenly on the outskirts, donger gangs would do battle against each other. The brawls looked like the Battle of Thermopylae. Finally the teacher on playground duty would plunge into the mêlée and send everyone in possession of a donger up to the deputy headmaster to get six. With me hovering elsewhere, solo desperadoes would then creep up on their victims behind the teacher's back. The idea was to clobber the target and be walking in the opposite direction with the donger in your pocket before the teacher turned around. He always turned around because the sound of the donger hitting someone's head was unmistakable. It sounded like an apple hitting concrete.

I was very keen not to be among those victimized. It followed that I should become one of those doing the victimizing. To this end I built a donger and chose the target likely to win me the most fame. At one point in the circumference of the playground there was a low picket fence separating the boys' primary school from the girls' primary school. It was forbidden to linger at this fence. I noticed a girl using the fence as a whippy. She was leaning against it with her face buried in her folded arms while other girls hid. If some other girl got to the whippy while she was away searching, there would be a cry of 'All in, the whippy's taken.' But at the moment she was still busy counting to a hundred, I came at her in a long curving run, swinging the donger like a sling. Contact was perfect. She dropped as though poleaxed – which, to all intents and purposes, she had been. I ran right into the teacher's arms.

And so I kept my feared but wished-for appointment with the deputy headmaster. He was a tall, slim man in a grey dust-coat. I can't remember his name, but I can well remember his quietly sardonic manner. He pointed out to me that in hitting the little girl I had caused her pain, and that he was now about to show me what pain was like. The instrument I had employed on the little girl had been strictly banned. The same embargo, he explained, did not apply to the instrument he would now employ on me. I was inspecting this while he spoke. It was a long, thick cane with a leather-bound tip. Unlike other canes I had seen, it did not seem to be flexible. Instead of swishing when it came down, it hummed. The impact was like a door slamming on my hand. I was too stunned even to pee my pants. The same thing happened to the other hand. Then the same thing again happened to each hand twice more in succession. That would teach me, he informed me, to hit little girls with dongers.

If he meant that it would teach me *not* to hit little girls with dongers, he was right. For one thing, I couldn't have lifted a donger, let alone swung one. When I tried to feed myself my play-lunch sandwiches, I kept missing my mouth. But at least the fame accruing to the maximum penalty had raised my status somewhat. I was never admitted to the inner circle of Kenny Mears, the school's most impressive bully. But for a while I was not so often among those bullied. Probably I was lucky not to be included among the oppressors. I admired Mears, but for his self-possession more than for his capacity to inflict suffering. He was completely without fear. Like Napoleon or Hitler, he seemed imaginative through having no idea of natural limits to his actions. He was a sawn-off Siegfried, a Nietzschean superman in short pants. He embodied Gibbon's definition of the barbarian, since his liberty was to indulge the whim of the moment, and his courage was to ignore the consequences. He was a frightful little shit.

But he had the kind of poise that I have always envied. He swore at the teachers man-to-man and could absorb an infinite amount of punishment without batting an eye. Indeed he never even blinked. Playing marbles, he made Mick Roach look like the Marquis of Queensberry. Mears fudged unblushingly. Wittgenstein defined a game as consisting of the rules by which it is played. If he had seen Mears in action, he would have realized that a game is further defined by what the dominant player can get away with. The basic rule of marbles is that the taw must be fired from outside the ring. If the firing hand creeps inside the ring before the moment of release, it's a fudge. Mears fudged more blatantly than his helpless opponents would have believed possible. Standing up instead of crouching down, he fell forward until his firing hand was almost touching the dates. Then he released his taw. The dates sang out of the ring and into his keeping. If anybody protested, violence would ensue. Nor was anyone allowed not to play. Years later I saw the film of *Guys and Dolls*. There is a famous scene where Nathan Detroit's floating crap-game moves to the sewers, and Big Julie from Chicago proposes to roll his own dice, which have no spots. When challenged, he produces a .45 automatic. I thought immediately: 'Mears.'

Mears's favourite means of persuasion was the Chinese burn. Grasping your hand in one of his, he would twist your wrist with the other. After having this done to me by boys older and bigger, I sought revenge by doing it to boys younger and smaller. But I quickly found out that I was naturally averse to being cruel. Reading the *Wide World* magazines, I had been excited by a chapter dealing with torture chambers. I still find it disturbing that sex and cruelty should be connected somewhere in my instincts. But the human personality is a drama, not a monologue; sad tricks of the mind can be offset by sound feelings in the heart; and the facts say that I have always been revolted by the very idea of deliberately causing pain. Considering the amount of pain I have been able to cause without meaning to, I suppose this is not much of a defence, but to me it has always seemed an important point. I burned a lot of sugar-ants with my magnifying glass, but if the sugar-ants had spoken to me as they might have spoken to St Francis, I would have desisted soon enough. Having a character that consists mainly of defects, I try to correct them one by one, but there are limits to the altitude that can be attained by hauling on one's own boot-straps. One is what one is, and if one isn't very nice or good, then it brings some solace to remember that other men have been worse. At various times in my life I have tried to pose as a thug, but the imposture has always collapsed of its own accord. I could be coerced into hurting other people. I have done it by chance often enough. But I could never enjoy it.

At home things were a bit easier than at school. Once or twice

I announced my intention of running away, but my mother defused the threat by packing me a bag containing peanut-butter sandwiches and pyjamas. The first time I got no further than the top of our street and was back home within the hour. The second time I got all the way to Rocky Point Road, more than two hundred yards from home. I was not allowed to cross Rocky Point Road. But I sat there until sunset. Otherwise I did my escaping symbolically, tunnelling into the poultry farm and surfacing among the chooks with a crumbling cap of birdshit on my head.

The teacher's pet image would have followed me home if my mother had had her way. She had a deadly habit of inviting the neighbours in for tea so that she could casually refer to my school reports a couple of hundred times. The most favoured recipient of these proud tirades was Nola Huthnance, who lived four doors down. Nola Huthnance was no mean talker herself, being joint holder, with her next-door neighbour Gail Thorpe, of the local record for yapping across the back fence – an unbeatable lunch-to-sunset epic during which there was no point at which one or the other was not talking and very few moments when both were not talking simultaneously. But not even Nola Huthnance could hold her own when my mother got going on the subject of her wonderful son and his outstanding intelligence. Long after I had been sent to bed, I would lurk in the hall listening to my mother extolling my virtues in the lounge room. Apparently Gogol's mother was under the impression that her son had invented the printing press and the steam engine. My own mother thought along roughly the same lines. I lapped it all up, but could see even at the time that such talk would do me no good with the locals, unless I cultivated a contrary reputation on my own account.

Luckily, whether by being just the right age or by having more than my fair share of productive neuroses, I continued to think up the kind of games that most of the other children in Margaret Street were keen to get in on. Wet weather put an end to the tunnelling season, but it produced flooded gutters. In those days proper concrete kerbing had not yet been laid down. Water flowed down erratic gutters through the width of bare earth and clay between the front strip and the ragged-edged asphalt road. Swollen with rain, these gutters were ripe for having sticks and plastic boats raced down them. At the top of Margaret Street, beyond the T-junction with Irene Street, was a block of waste ground known as the quarry. Probably the convicts had once hacked stone there – Botany Bay was only about a mile to the east. The fall of ground from the back to the front of the block was only fifteen feet or so but to us it looked like Annapurna. In wet weather the water poured down the exposed rock face of the quarry and formed streamlets begging to be dammed. I used to build whole networks of mud dams, fanatically smoothing them off and facing them with pieces of fibro, so that they resembled the photographs of the Boulder and Grand Coulee dams in my *Modern Marvels Encyclopedia*. In the lakes formed by the dams I built harbours for plastic boats. Liberated from the confines of the bath, they could be pushed around in a more interesting seascape than that bounded by my soapy knees. There were secret bases under tufts of over-hanging grass. Holding my face close to a boat as I pushed it, I could study the bow waves and the wake. The boats were only a few inches long but they looked like the *Bismarck* if you got near enough. I built roads along the docks and up through the foothills. Plastic, lead and tin toy cars could be pushed along them. Dinky Toys were rare at that time. A Triang Minic jeep – later lost, to my mother's anguished disgust – was the star turn. Wound up, it could make progress even through mud. Other vehicles had to be pushed. With them it was all pretend.

But it was pretend in ideal surroundings. Other children brought their boats and cars, blundering into my ashlared revet-ments, gouging crude paths, botching together laughable garages and ludicrous U-boat pens. At first I told them to go and build their own dams. Then I resigned myself to having my work ruined. At the small price of an offence to my aesthetic instincts, I was able to rule the roost. Besides, with cheap labour available my schemes could be allowed to wax ever grander. Like Themistocles linking

Athens with Piraeus, I walled in the whole area. My designs assumed the proportions of Karnak or Speer's Berlin. I was the overseer, the construction boss, the superintendent of works. But even when my loyal slaves were toiling away in every direction, I would sometimes relapse into a detailed concern for a certain stretch of road or dockside, smoothing it endlessly with the edge of my hand into an ever sweeter curve or sharper edge.

None of this meant that I was a good practical hand. For example, I could not build billycarts very well. Other children, most of them admittedly older than I, but some of them infuriatingly not, constructed billycarts of advanced design, with skeletal hard-wood frames and steel-jacketed ball-race wheels that screamed on the concrete footpaths like a diving Stuka. The best I could manage was a sawn-off fruit box mounted on a fence-paling spine frame, with drearily silent rubber wheels taken off an old pram. In such a creation I could go at a reasonable clip down our street and twice as fast down Sunbeam Avenue, which was much steeper at the top. But even going down Sunbeam my billycart was no great thrill compared with the ball-race models, which having a ground-clearance of about half an inch and being almost frictionless were able to attain tremendous velocities at low profile, so that to the onlooker their riders seemed to be travelling downhill sitting magically just above the ground, while to the riders themselves the sense of speed was breathtaking.

After school and at weekends boys came from all over the district to race on the Sunbeam Avenue footpaths. There would be twenty or thirty carts, two-thirds of them with ball-races. The noise was indescribable. It sounded like the Battle of Britain going on in somebody's bathroom. There would be about half an hour's racing before the police came. Residents often took the law into their own hands, hosing the grim-faced riders as they went shrieking by. Sunbeam Avenue ran parallel to Margaret Street but it started higher and lasted longer. Carts racing down the footpath on the far side had a straight run of about a quarter of a mile all the way to the park. Emitting shockwaves of sound, the ball-race carts would

attain such speeds that it was impossible for the rider to get off. All
he could do was to crash reasonably gently when he got to the end.
Carts racing down the footpath on the near side could go only half
as far, although very nearly as fast, before being faced with a right-
angle turn into Irene Street. Here a pram-wheeled cart like mine
could demonstrate its sole advantage. The traction of the rubber
tyres made it possible to negotiate the corner in some style. I
developed a histrionic lean-over of the body and slide of the back
wheels which got me around the corner unscathed, leaving black
smoking trails of burnt rubber. Mastery of this trick saved me from
being relegated to the ranks of the little kids, than which there was
no worse fate. I had come to depend on being thought of as a big
kid. Luckily only the outstanding ball-race drivers could match my
fancy turn into Irene Street. Others slid straight on with a yelp of
metal and a shower of sparks, braining themselves on the asphalt
road. One driver scalped himself under a bread van.

The Irene Street corner was made doubly perilous by Mrs
Branthwaite's poppies. Mrs Branthwaite inhabited the house on the
corner. She was a known witch whom we often persecuted after
dark by throwing gravel on her roof. It was widely believed she
poisoned cats. Certainly she was a great ringer-up of the police. In
retrospect I can see that she could hardly be blamed for this, but
her behaviour seemed at the time like irrational hatred of children.
She was a renowned gardener. Her front yard was like the cover of
a seed catalogue. Extending her empire, she had flower beds even
on her two front strips, one on the Sunbeam Avenue side and the
other on the Irene Street side – i.e., on both outside edges of the
famous corner. The flower beds held the area's best collection of
poppies. She had been known to phone the police if even one of
these was illicitly picked.

At the time I am talking about, Mrs Branthwaite's poppies
were all in bloom. It was essential to make the turn without hurting a single hair of a poppy's head, otherwise the old lady would
probably drop the telephone and come out shooting. Usually, when

the poppies were in bloom, nobody dared make the turn. I did – not out of courage, but because in my ponderous cart there was no real danger of going wrong. The daredevil leanings-over and the dramatic skids were just icing on the cake.

I should have left it at that, but got ambitious. One Saturday afternoon when there was a particularly large turnout, I got sick of watching the ball-race carts howling to glory down the far side. I organized the slower carts like my own into a train. Every cart except mine was deprived of its front axle and loosely bolted to the cart in front. The whole assembly was about a dozen carts long, with a big box cart at the back. This back cart I dubbed the chuck wagon, using terminology I had picked up from the Hopa-long Cassidy serial at the pictures. I was the only one alone on his cart. Behind me there were two or even three to every cart until you got to the chuck wagon, which was crammed full of little kids, some of them so small that they were holding toy koalas and sucking dummies.

From its very first run down the far side, my super-cart was a triumph. Even the adults who had been hosing us called their families out to marvel as we went steaming by. On the super-cart's next run there was still more to admire, since even the top-flight ball-race riders had demanded to have their vehicles built into it, thereby heightening its tone, swelling its passenger list and multi-plying its already impressive output of decibels. Once again I should have left well alone. The thing was already famous. It had everything but a dining car. Why did I ever suggest that we should transfer it to the near side and try the Irene Street turn?

With so much inertia the super-cart started slowly, but it accelerated like a piano falling out of a window. Long before we reached the turn I realized that there had been a serious miscalcu-lation. The miscalculation was all mine, of course. Sir Isaac Newton would have got it right. It was too late to do anything except pray. Leaning into the turn, I skidded my own cart safely around in the usual way. The next few segments followed me, but with each segment describing an arc of slightly larger radius than the one in front. First gradually, then with stunning finality, the monster lashed its enormous tail.

The air was full of flying ball-bearings, bits of wood, big kids, little kids, koalas and dummies. Most disastrously of all, it was also full of poppy petals. Not a bloom escaped the scythe. Those of us who could still run scattered to the winds, dragging our wounded with us. The police spent hours visiting all the parents in the district, warning them that the billycart era was definitely over. It was a police car that took Mrs Branthwaite away. There was no point waiting for the ambulance. She could walk all right. It was just that she couldn't talk. She stared straight ahead, her mouth slightly open.

4. THE FORCE OF DESTRUCTION

Such catastrophes distressed my mother but she wrote them off as growing pains. Other exploits broke her heart. Once when she was out shopping I was riding my second-hand Malvern Star 26-inch-frame bicycle around the house on a complicated circuit which led from the backyard along the driveway, once around a small fir tree that stood in the front yard, and back along the narrow side passage. Passing boys noticed what I was up to and came riding in. In a while there were a dozen or so of us circulating endlessly against the clock. Once again I could not leave well alone. I organized a spectacular finish in which the riders had to plunge into my mother's prize privet hedge. The idea was for the bike's front wheel to lodge in the thick privet and the rider to fall dramatically into the bush and disappear. It became harder and harder to disappear as the privet became more and more reduced to ruins.

Giddy with success, I started doing the same thing to the hydrangeas. Finally I did it to the fir tree, ramming it with the bike and falling through it, thereby splitting its trunk. When my mother came wearily down the street with the shopping she must have thought the house had been strafed. I was hiding under it – a sure sign of advanced guilt and fear, since it was dark under there and red-backs were plentiful. She chased me up the peach tree and hit me around the ankles with a willow wand. It didn't hurt me as much as her tears did. Not for the only time, I heard her tell me that I was more than she could cope with. I suppose there was a possibility that I somehow felt compelled to go on reminding her of that fact.

Bombing my bed didn't make me very popular either. It was a trick I learned while recovering from mumps. Climbing onto the top of the wardrobe in my room, I would jump off and land on my bed, which seemed an immense distance below. Actually it was only a few feet, but the bed groaned satisfactorily. Eventually there were half a dozen of us climbing up and jumping off in rapid succession. It was a mistake to let Graham Truscott play. He had a double chin even at that age and a behind like a large bag of soil. But it took him so long to climb the wardrobe that it seemed unreasonable not to let him jump off it. The frame of the bed snapped off its supports with the noise of a firing squad and crashed to the floor with the roar of cannon. I sent everyone home and tried to restore the bed to its right height by putting suitcases under it, but all that did was cave in the suitcases. Once again it was very dark under the house.

And once again there was an element of panic in my mother's fury. It sprang, of course, from the fact that what we owned was all we had. My mother had a war widow's pension to bring me up on. It wasn't much. The Returned Servicemen's League, always known as the RSL, was a formidable pressure group in the post-war years but those servicemen who had not returned exerted no pressure at all. The Legacy Club threw a Christmas party every year. Otherwise the bereaved wives were paid off mainly in rhetoric, most of it emanating from the silver tongue of Robert Gordon Menzies, alias Ming, who went on being Prime Minister for what seemed like eternity. My mother never failed to vote for him. She had quite a lot of political nous, but Ming's patrician style numbed her judgement. Thus she went on remaining loyal to the Liberal Party, while the Liberal Party went on ensuring that her pension would never be so lavish as to encourage idleness.

She eked out her pittance by smocking babies' dresses. The smocking was done on a brick wrapped in cloth. The panel to be smocked was threaded on a long pin and the pin was in turn pushed through the cloth along the top edge of the brick. Then with a needle and thread she produced row after row of tiny stitches, the stitches forming exquisite patterns on the pink or blue cloth. She was paid piece rates. They were not high. She worked pretty well all day and often far into the evening while we listened to the radio. She would stop only for Jack Davey, who we were agreed was a great wit. Bob Dyer she found ridiculous, but listened to him just so that she could loathe him. After I went to bed she often went on working. Once a week she took the finished pieces up to the woman in Oatley who assembled the dresses. The round trip took the whole day. It was often during these absences that I perpetrated my worst crimes, such as the bed-wrecking incident. Right back at the very start, almost the first week we were in Kogarah, I distinguished myself by helping to restore the colour in a faded patch of the lounge-room carpet. I did this by rubbing a whole tin of Nugget dark tan boot-polish into the deprived area. By the time she got back from Oatley I was already in pre-emptive tears, having divined that the results did not look quite right. On such occasions she looked beyond anger, manifesting a sort of resigned desperation.

Gradually I learned that damaging anything around the house produced more emotional wear and tear than I could deal with. So I started damaging things away from the house. I became adept at knocking out street lights. There was plenty of gravel lying around at the edge of the road. After dusk I could bend down, pick up a stone, flick it up at the light, and be halfway home before the pieces of shattered bulb hit the ground. These were small-time depredations but they led on to bigger things.

Every Saturday afternoon at the pictures there was a feature film, sixteen cartoons and an episode each from four different serials. The programme just went on and on like Bayreuth. The Margaret Street children would join up with the Irene Street children and the combined mass would add themselves unto the Sunbeam Avenue children and the aggregate would join the swarm of children from all the other areas all moving north along Rocky Point Road towards Rockdale, where the Odeon stood. In summer the concrete footpaths were hot. The asphalt footpaths were even hotter: bubbles of tar formed, to be squashed flat by our leathery bare feet. Running around on macadamized playgrounds throughout the spring, by summer we had feet that could tread on a drawing pin and hardly feel it.

When you got to the Odeon the first thing you did was stock up with lollies. Lollies was the word for what the English call sweets and the Americans call candy. Some of the more privileged children had upwards of five shillings each to dispose of, but in fact two bob was enough to buy you as much as you could eat. Everyone, without exception, bought at least one Hoadley's Violet Crumble Bar. It was a slab of dense, dry honeycomb coated with chocolate. So frangible was the honeycomb that it would shatter when bitten, scattering bright yellow shrapnel. It was like trying to eat a Ming vase. The honeycomb would go soft only after a day's exposure to direct sunlight. The chocolate surrounding it, however, would liquefy after only ten minutes in a dark cinema.

Fantails came in a weird blue rhomboidal packet shaped like an isosceles triangle with one corner missing. Each individual Fantail was wrapped in a piece of paper detailing a film star's biography – hence the pun, fan tales. The Fantail itself was a chocolate-coated toffee so glutinous that it could induce lockjaw in a mule. People had to have their mouths chipped open with a cold chisel. One packet of Fantails would last an average human being for ever. A group of six small boys could go through a packet during the course of a single afternoon at the pictures, but it took hard work and involved a lot of strangled crying in the dark. Any fillings you had in your second teeth would be removed instantly, while children who still had any first teeth left didn't keep them long.

The star lolly, outstripping even the Violet Crumble Bar and the Fantail in popularity, was undoubtedly the Jaffa. A packet of Jaffas was loaded like a cluster bomb with about fifty globular lollies the size of ordinary marbles. The Jaffa had a dark chocolate core and a brittle orange candy coat: in cross-section it looked rather like the planet Earth. It presented two alternative ways of being eaten, each with its allure. You could fondle the Jaffa on the tongue until your saliva ate its way through the casing, whereupon the taste of chocolate would invade your mouth with a sublime, majestic inevitability. Or you could bite straight through and submit the interior of your head to a stunning explosion of flavour. Sucking and biting your way through forty or so Jaffas while Jungle Jim wrestled with the crocodiles, you nearly always had a few left over after the stomach could take no more. The spare Jaffas made ideal ammunition. Flying through the dark, they would bounce off an infantile skull with the noise of bullets hitting a bell. They showered on the stage when the manager came out to announce the lucky ticket. The Jaffa is a part of Australia's theatrical heritage. There was a famous occasion, during the Borovansky Ballet production of *Giselle* at the Tivoli in Sydney, when Albrecht was forced to abandon the performance. It was a special afternoon presentation of the ballet before an audience of schoolchildren. Lying in a swoon while awaiting the reappearance of Giselle, Albrecht aroused much comment because of his protuberant codpiece. After being hit square on the power-bulge by a speeding Jaffa, he woke up with a rush and hopped off the stage in the stork position.

Everyone either ate steadily or raced up and down the aisles to and from the toilet, or all three. The uproar was continuous, like Niagara. Meanwhile the programme was unreeling in front of us. The feature film was usually a Tarzan, a Western, or the kind of Eastern Western in which George Macready played the grand vizier. At an even earlier stage I had been to the pictures with my mother and been continuously frightened without understanding what was going on – the mere use of music to reinforce tension, for example, was enough to drive me under the seat for the rest of the evening. At a later stage I accompanied my mother to every change of evening double bill both at Ramsgate and Rockdale – a total of four films a week, every week for at least a decade. But nothing before or since had the impact of those feature films at the Rockdale Saturday matinees.

In those days Johnny Weissmuller was making his difficult transition from Tarzan to Jungle Jim. As Tarzan he got fatter and fatter until finally he was too fat to be plausible, whereupon he was obliged to put on a safari suit and become Jungle Jim. I was glad to learn subsequently that as Jungle Jim he had a piece of the action and was at last able to bank some money. At the time, his transmogrification looked to me like an unmitigated tragedy. His old Tarzan movies were screened again and again. Many times I dived with Tarz off Brooklyn Bridge during the climactic scene of *Tarzan's New York Adventure*. In my mind I duplicated the back somersaults executed by Johnny's double as he swung from vine to vine on his way to rescue the endangered Jane and Boy from the invading ivory hunters. In one of the Tarzan movies there is a terrible sequence where one lot of natives gives another lot an extremely thin time by arranging pairs of tree trunks so that they will fly apart and pull the victim to pieces. This scene stayed with me as a paradigm of evil. No doubt if I saw the same film today I would find the sequence as crudely done as everything else ever filmed on Poverty Row. But at the time it seemed a vision of cruelty too horrible even to think about.

I can remember having strong ideas about which cartoons were funny and which were not. Mr Magoo and Gerald McBoing-Boing, with their stylized backgrounds and elliptical animation, had not yet arrived on the scene. Cartoons were still in that hyper-realist phase which turns out in retrospect to have been their golden age. The standards of animation set by Walt Disney and MGM cost a lot of time, effort and money, but as so often happens the art reached its height at the moment of maximum resistance from the medium. Knowing nothing of these theoretical matters, I simply consumed the product. I knew straight away that the Tom and Jerry cartoons were the best. In fact I even knew straight away that some Tom and Jerry cartoons were better than others. There was an early period when Tom's features were puffy and he ran with a lope, motion being indicated by the streaks that animators call speed lines. In the later period Tom's features had an acute precision and his every move was made fully actual, with no stylization at all. Meanwhile Jerry slimmed down and acquired more expressiveness. The two periods were clearly separated in my mind, where they were dubbed 'old drawings' and 'new drawings'. I remember being able to tell which category a given Tom and Jerry cartoon fell into from seeing the first few frames. Eventually I could tell just from the logo. I remember clearly the feeling of disappointment if it was going to be old drawings and the feeling of elation if it was going to be new drawings.

But the serials were what caught my imagination most, especially the ones in which the hero was masked. It didn't occur to me until much later that the producers, among whom Sam Katzman was the doyen, kept the heroes masked so that the leading actors could not ask for more money. At the time it just seemed logical to me that a hero should wear a mask. It didn't have to be as elaborate as Batman's mask. I admired Batman, despite the worrying wrinkles in the arms and legs of his costume, which attained a satisfactory tautness only in the region of his stomach. But Robin's mask was easier to copy. So was the Black Commando's. My favourite serials were those in which masked men went out at night and melted mysteriously into the urban landscape. Science-fiction serials were less appealing at that stage, while white hunter epics like *The Lost City of the Jungle* merely seemed endless. I saw all fourteen episodes of *The Lost City of the Jungle* except the last. It would have made no difference if I had seen only the last episode and missed the thirteen leading up to it. The same things happened every week. Either two parties of white hunters in solar topees searched for each other in one part of the jungle, or else the same two parties of white hunters in solar topees sought to avoid each other in another part of the jungle. Meanwhile tribesmen from the Lost City either captured representatives of both parties and took them to the high priestess for sacrifice, or else ran after them when they escaped. Sometimes white hunters escaping ran into other white hunters being captured, and were either recaptured or helped the others escape. It was obvious even to my unschooled eye that there was only about half an acre of jungle, all of it composed of papier mâché. By the end of each episode it was beaten flat. The screen would do a spiral wipe around an image of the enthroned high priestess, clad in a variety of tea towels and gesturing obdurately with a collection of prop sceptres while one of the good white hunters – you could tell a good one from a bad one by the fact that a bad one always sported a very narrow moustache – was lowered upside down into a pit of limp scorpions.

Exotic locations left me cold. What I liked was the idea of possessing unlimited powers and yet blending undetectably into everyday life, although not so undetectably that ordinary people would not be able to tell at a glance who I was. The trouble with Superman, Captain Marvel, Captain Marvel Jr., Batman and the rest of the dual-identity squad was that no one thought much of them when they were in mufti. Lois Lane practically wore her lip out sneering at Clark Kent while the poor drongo stood there and took it. Billy Batson was always getting his crutch kicked. Bruce Wayne was derided as a playboy. None of that happened to me. Discreetly informing people one by one, I made sure everybody in the district knew that when dusk descended it was I, and nobody else, who became the Flash of Lightning.

5. ENTER THE FLASH OF LIGHTNING

Thus there was no fruitless speculation about my real identity as I streaked past in my green felt mask and black cape. Like Dracula, the Flash of Lightning made his appearance only after nightfall. In the hours between sunset and bedtime an imposing figure could be seen outlined against the stars. In less time than it took to pronounce his name in an awed whisper, he was gone, running down one side of the street and up the other, darting along driveways, clambering over back fences and making his inexorable progress from backyard to backyard. You would not have known, when this sinister avatar caught and slipped your startled gaze, that his mask and cape had been made by his mother.

Actually the Flash of Lightning's cape was almost his undoing. It was fastened at his neck by two short lengths of rope tied in a bow. Flitting awkwardly homeward over our backyard fence one night, I got the rope tangled around the top of a paling. The result should have been death by strangulation. There was a frantic, wordless struggle in which the Flash of Lightning's proverbial dignity was overwhelmed by a mortal urge to breathe. Just when it looked like curtains for the Flash of Lightning, the cape popped a seam and I dropped vertically into the choco patch.

But such failures were few. Generally the Flash of Lightning was a success. Other boys started appearing in masks and capes. Moments after the sun dropped they would come swooping towards me like fruit bats. Obviously everything was up to me. Standing around in mysterious attire, surrogates of the Flash of Lightning awaited their instructions. Meanwhile they announced their names. There was a Green Flash, a Black Flash and a Red

Flash. Graham Truscott wanted to call himself the Flash of Thunder. I took pity on them all and gave them their assignments. These started off as harmless games of doorbell-ringing but became less cute with time. Throwing gravel on Mrs Branthwaite's roof must have been agony for her, even though it was endlessly amusing to us. Films of Kristallnacht never fail to make me think of those brilliantly staged raids by the Flash of Lightning, in which a dozen handfuls of gravel would all land on Mrs Branthwaite's tiles only seconds before the perpetrators, magically divested of capes and masks, were back at home sitting around the Kosi stove and helping their parents listen to *Pick a Box*. The difference between mischief and murder is no greater than what the law will allow. All we were allowed, thank God, was mischief – and in retrospect that looks bad enough.

What I had going, of course, was a gang. Only lack of opportunity saved us from outright delinquency. There was a limit to what destruction we could cause, but everything within that limit sooner or later got done. Overwhelming temptation was provided by a sudden increase in the number of building sites. The bottom half of the street, towards the park, had previously been vacant blocks. These were suddenly all built on at once by the Housing Commission. The plan was to provide a lot of new houses in a tearing hurry. People at the top of the street started sneering at the people at the bottom of the street before the people at the bottom of the street had even moved in. Adults were agreed that this sudden influx would lower the tone. By night, and even by day if conditions were favourable, the Flash of Lightning and his gang made sure that work on the building sites proceeded as slowly as possible.

It is remarkable how much damage a group of small boys can do to a building site if it is left unguarded. In loose moments I might pride myself on possessing a creative impulse but I don't have to do too much introspection before being forced to admit that a destructive impulse is in there somewhere as well. Under my supervision, dumps of mixed lime were well seeded with bricks. A brick dropped from high up into soft lime makes a very satisfactory glurp. Studded with bricks like ice cream full of chipped chocolate, the lime quickly became unusable. We smashed tiles by the hundred. Porcelain lavatory bowls were reduced to their constituent molecules. Timber frames stood upright, waiting for brick walls to be formed around them. Using an umbrella as a parachute, the Flash of Lightning could jump from the top of one of these frames and land in a sandpit. Or the Flash of Lightning thought he could. The Flash of Lightning was lucky to land perfectly flat, so that he was merely winded instead of crippled for life.

That put a temporary end to my share in the marauding. But if we had all gone out every night and worked until dawn taking apart everything that had been put together, transformation would still have been inevitable. The district was changing. The poultry farm was sold up and subdivided into blocks of building land. Irene Street was extended through it, to join up with a new road called Madrers Avenue, so that there were now two ways up to Rocky Point Road. This must have happened in fits and starts over the course of years, but I remember it as a surge of innovation. Concrete kerbing was laid down, so that everybody's front strip had two edges to be kept sharply defined instead of one. Most sensational change of all, the sewer came. Vast trenches were dug in which pipes were laid. My mother boldly proposed that one of the miraculous new devices should be installed not only in the outside lavatory but in the bathroom itself. The very notion spelled doom for the dunny man.

Ever since I could remember, the dunny man had come running down the driveway once a week. From inside the house, we could hear his running footsteps. Then we could hear the rattle and thump as he lifted the lavatory, took out the full pan, clipped on a special lid and set down an empty pan in its place. After more rattling and banging, there was an audible intake of breath as he hefted the full pan onto his shoulder. Then the footsteps went back along the driveway, slower this time but still running. From outside in the street there was rattling, banging and shouting as the full pan was loaded onto the dunny cart along with all the other full pans. I often watched the dunny cart from the front window. As it slowly made its noisome way down the street, the dunny men ran to and from it with awesome expertise. They wore shorts, sandshoes and nothing else except a suntan suspiciously deep on the forearms. Such occasional glimpses were all one was allowed by one's parents and all that was encouraged even by the dunny men themselves. They preferred to work in nobody's company except their own. They were a band apart.

Years went by without those running footsteps being acknowledged by any other means except a bottle of beer left standing in the lavatory on the closest visiting day to Christmas Day. Otherwise it seemed generally agreed that the lavatory pan was changed by magic. From day to day it got fuller and fuller, generating maggots by about the third day. To combat the smell, honeysuckle was grown on a trellis outside the lavatory door, in the same way that the European nobility had recourse to perfume when they travelled by galley. The maggots came from blowflies and more blowflies came from the maggots. Blowflies were called blowies. The Australian climate, especially on the eastern seaboard in the latitude of Sydney, was specifically designed to accommodate them. The blowies' idea of a good time was to hang around the dunny waiting for the seat to be lifted. They were then faced with the challenge of getting through the hole before it was blocked by the descending behind of the prospective occupant. There was no time for any fancy flying. Whether parked on the wall or stacked around in a holding pattern near the ceiling, every blowie was geared up to make either a vertical dive from high altitude or a death-defying low-level run through the rapidly decreasing airspace between the seat and your descending arse. The moment the seat came up, suddenly it was Pearl Harbor.

Once inside, enclosed under a dark sky, the blowies set about dumping their eggs. The memory of the results has always, in my mind, given extra vividness to Shakespeare's line about life in excrements. God knows what would have happened if ever the dunny men had gone on strike. Even as things were, by the end of the week the contents of the pan would be getting too close for comfort. Luckily the dunny man was a model of probity. Never putting a foot wrong, he carried out his Sisyphean task in loyal silence. Only when he was about to leave our lives for ever did his concentration slip. Perhaps he foresaw that one day the sewer would come to everywhere in the world. Perhaps, in order to ward off these grim thoughts, he partook of his Christmas beer while still engaged in the task. Because it was on that day – the day before Christmas Eve – that the dunny man made his solitary mistake.

My mother and I were having breakfast. I heard the dunny man's footsteps thumping along the driveway, with a silent pause as he hurdled my bicycle, which in my habitual carelessness I had left lying there. I heard the usual thumps, bangs and heaves. I could picture the brimming pan, secured with the special clipped lid, hoisted high on his shoulder while he held my mother's gift bottle of beer in his other, appreciative hand. Then the footsteps started running back the other way. Whether he forgot about my bicycle, or simply mistimed his jump, there was no way of telling. Suddenly there was the noise of . . . well, it was mainly the noise of a dunny man running full tilt into a bicycle. The uproar was made especially ominous by the additional noise – tiny but significant in context – of a clipped lid springing off.

While my mother sat there with her hands over her eyes I raced out through the fly-screen door and took a look down the drive-way. The dunny man, overwhelmed by the magnitude of his tragedy, had not yet risen to his feet. Needless to say, the contents of the pan had been fully divulged. All the stuff had come out. But what was really remarkable was the way none of it had missed him. Already you could hear a gravid hum in the air. Millions of flies were on their way towards us. They were coming from all over Australia. For them, it was a Durbar, a moot, a gathering of the clans. For us, it was the end of an era.

Once the new lavatories were installed, the bathroom became

the centre of all ablutions. I no longer took a book to the outside lavatory and sat absorbed, the door thrown open to admit light. Just as well, because towards the end of the unsewered epoch I was caught in that position by Valma Chappelow, the girl from across the road. She was older than I was too, which made it worse. She came pounding around the corner of the house on her way to borrow something that her scatter-brained mother had forgotten to buy when out shopping – bread, butter, milk, meat or some other frippery like that. Valma got a good look at me sitting there with my pants around my ankles. She made sure everybody in the district got to hear about it. She told her pen-pals. Years later at a party in Caringbah, more than twenty miles away by train, I met a stranger who knew all about it. If I went to live in the Outer Hebrides I would probably find the inhabitants all giggling behind their hands.

But the district didn't change as much as it stayed the same. As I grew older, my picture of where I lived grew wider and more complicated. The expanding of one's vision is usually enough in itself to generate a feeling that everything is falling apart. Nevertheless one had a sense of constancy even at the time, and looking back on it I can see that my whole childhood was remarkable for the amount of entertainment permanently on flow. All you had to do was turn the tap and bend your pursed lips to the bubbler.

Admittedly some of the local adults were terrifying. Gail Thorpe's husband Wally was a pastry cook whose business had failed. His principal means of revenge was to browbeat his wife, who went away for electric-convulsion therapy every year or so. The only result of the treatment was to alter the position of her nervous smile, so that instead of being on the front of her face it ended up under one ear. By the time it drifted around to the front again she was ready for another course of treatment. Wally also tormented his children in various ways. He would go on tickling his younger daughter, Carmel, long after the desperately sobbing child had begged him to stop. Watching these perform-ances, I woke up early to the reality of human evil. News of mass political atrocity has always saddened me but never come as a surprise. The only time I tried to interfere with one of Wally Thorpe's divertissements, he swore at me for ten minutes on end at the top of his voice. I went home stunned. My mother did her best to tell him off but it was clear that at such moments she sorely felt her loneliness. That night was one of the few times I ever heard her say, 'I wish your father had come home.'

The Goodhews were likewise a bit of a pain. They were so protective about their sons, Darryl and Des, that they would trail them about, checking up on what was going on. This could be awkward when what was going on was a full-scale battle involving the throwing of stones and bits of fibro. These battles usually took place up in the quarry, with the defenders occupying foxholes in the heights and the attackers moving up through the lowlands from one clump of lantana to another. Very properly concerned about their children losing an eye, the Goodhew parents would invariably show up just in time to see one of their little darlings sconed by a rock or sliced open by a whizzing piece of fibro. The fuss would take weeks to die down. According to Mr and Mrs Goodhew, their children were being led astray by the local toughs. In fact their own progeny were the worst of the lot. Darryl Goodhew could look wonderfully innocent when his parents were around, but he was a dead shot when they weren't looking. He once knocked Beverley Hindmarsh off her dinkey at an incredible range. The missile was a lump of sandstone. He was sharing a foxhole with me at the top of the quarry. It was the best foxhole: you had to crawl through a lantana tunnel to get to it. Halfway down Margaret Street, Beverley was a dot on the horizon when Darryl launched the rock. It was a long time on its way. I had lost sight of it long before she abruptly stopped pedalling and crashed sideways with awful finality. Darryl immediately ran towards the scene of the crime with a look of concern. His air of innocence was so persuasive that Beverley's parents never thought of blaming him. They would have blamed me if I had been stupid enough to emerge from the lantanas. I was already established as Beverley's persecutor, having pinched her

bottom one day with a metal reinforcing clip stolen from a building site. It was meant to be a joke, but it took a piece out of her
pointed behind. I got belted for that, and if I surfaced now I would
get belted again. Besides, Darryl would undoubtedly have pointed
the finger at me. So I stayed up there until the stars came out.
Beverley suffered nothing more severe than shock and a badly
bruised infantile bud. When you consider that the stone might just
as easily have removed an eyeball, you can see that we must have
had a guardian angel.

Otherwise the adults left us pretty much alone. On the weekends
we made our big expeditions to the pictures, the swamp or the
dump. In the afternoons and evenings after school we played in
the street. We played cock-a-lorum from one side of the street
to the other. We played a game with half a dozen sticks spaced out
along the front strip and you were allowed to take only one step
between every two sticks. You kept moving the sticks further and
further apart until nobody was left in except some visiting kid built
like a praying mantis. You had to do as many chin-ups as you
could on the box tree. There were complicated bike races around
the block. The older boys did a lot of elaborate riding up and down
in front of the girls, who used to sit in line on the Chappelows'
front fence. Warren Hartigan could sit on his bicycle backwards
and ride past very slowly. They stopped giggling when he did that.
Graham Truscott should never have tried it. A spoke from one of
the wheels went right through his calf.

We played hidings and countries. In countries you threw a
tennis ball in the air and ran, calling out the name of a country.
Each player had the name of a country. If your country was called,
you tried to catch the ball before it bounced, whereupon you could
throw it up again and call out somebody else's country. If you
only caught it on the bounce, you had to ... Forget it. The rules
went on and on. All that mattered was to throw the ball high.
Greg Brennan could put it into orbit. He lived next door but one.
Nobody lived very far away. We played on and on through the hot
afternoon into the brief dusk and the sudden nightfall. Towards

sunset the adults would appear on the front porches and start watering the lawn. They would tune the nozzles to a fine spray, which would drift in the air at the first breath of the summer wind that came every night. Usually it was a nor'easter. Sometimes it was the Southerly Buster. The Christmas beetles and cowboy beetles held jamborees around the street lights, battering themselves against the white enamel reflectors and falling into the street. They lay on their backs with their legs struggling. When you picked them up they pulsed with the frustrated strength of their clenched wing muscles.

Before there was the refrigerator there was the ice-chest. A block of ice was loaded into it every couple of days. If you left a bottle of lemonade on top of the block of ice the bottle would sink in and get deliciously cold. We weren't rich but we had meat three times a day, even if it had to be rabbit. Before myxomatosis was introduced, the Australian rabbit was a lightly built racing model that made excellent food. Only in a protein-rich country like Australia could such a marvellous beast be looked down on. Leftover rabbit legs could be put in the ice-chest after dinner and eaten for breakfast next day. Surrounded with cold white fat, they looked like maps of Greenland and tasted like a dryad's inner thigh.

When the watermelon man came there was more melon than anyone could eat. You scooped the lines of black seeds out with your crooked finger and bit a face-sized piece out of the cool, crisp, red, sweet slice. Chomping away until your ears were full of sugar. Slurping and snarling until there was hardly a trace of pink left on the white lining of the rind. There was a kind of drink-on-a-stick called the Skybomber – a tetrahedron of deep green, lime-flavoured water frozen so hard that its surface had no grain. You had to suck it for half an hour before it gave in and became friable. Then whole layers of it would come away sweetly and easily in your numb mouth, as if the molecules had been arranged in strata, like graphite. Every time I see that shade of green I think immediately of Skybombers.

I'm sure it was aesthetically justifiable for Proust to concentrate on his piece of cake, but in fact almost anything can take you back. There is a rhapsodic stretch about ice cream in *La Prisonnière* that proves the point exactly. He imagines his tongue shaping the ice creams of long ago, and suddenly all the past comes rushing back with authentically uncontrolled force. Elsewhere in the novel he keeps his memory on a tight rein. Herzen was closer to the truth when he said that every memory calls up a dozen others. The real miracle of Proust is the discipline with which he stemmed the flow. Everything is a madeleine.

6. DIB, DIB, DIB, DIB

Somewhere about this time I was in the Cubs. When the time came for graduation to the Scouts, I was not accepted, and thus became for the brief time before I tossed the whole thing in, the oldest Cub in the First Kogarah Wolf Cub Pack and probably the world. Lacking the precious gift of taciturnity, I could never achieve the grim face essential to success in paramilitary organizations. Considering this fatal flaw, it is remarkable how many of them I tried to get into. The Cubs were merely the first in a long line. My mother made my scarf. It had to be in First Kogarah colours – maroon with yellow piping. She made me a woggle out of leather. Every Cub had to have a woggle. It held your scarf on. As well as the woggle, there were special sock-tops – called something like fuggles – which always fell down. After you passed your Tenderfoot you got a wolf's head, or diggle, to wear on your cap. Also on the cap went a scraggle for each year of service. In addition to woggles, fuggles, diggles and scraggles, successful Cubs had the right, indeed obligation, to wear a whole collection of insignia and badges. The second in command of a sub-pack of six Cubs was called a Seconder and wore a yellow stripe on his sleeve. The commander of a sub-pack was called a Sixer and wore two stripes. A sixer in his final year would be so covered in decorations that promotion to the Scouts became a physical necessity, lest he expire under the weight.

Ruling over the whole pack was Akela. Her name was taken from *The Jungle Book*. She wore a brown uniform with a Scout hat. Otherwise she, too, was burdened down with woggles and fuggles. At the beginning of our weekly meetings, we Cubs would squat in

a circle and worship her. While squatting, we made wolf-head signs
with our fingers and pointed them at the floor. Then we chanted,
'Akela, we'll do our best. We'll dib dib dib dib. We'll dob dob
dob dob . . .' This routine was climaxed by a mass throwing back
of heads and emitting of supposedly vulpine howls. I used to get
through the dibbing and dobbing all right but during the howling
I usually rolled over backwards.

My lack of poise could possibly have stemmed from a never-to-
be-satisfied wonderment about what dibbing and dobbing might
actually consist of, but more probably it was just the result of an
overwhelming love for Akela. I adored her. A schoolteacher in real
life, she was a mother figure with none of the drawbacks. For her
own part, she must have found me a problem, since I trailed her
around everywhere. The theory of Scouting, or in this case Cub-
bing, was that boys should become independent through the
acquisition of woodcraft and related skills. All I ever learned was
how to attach myself to Akela's skirt. This made it hard for Akela
and Baloo to be alone. Baloo the Bear was a young adult King's
Scout who visited the pack once a month. Decorated like a
combination of Boris Godunov and General MacArthur, a King's
Scout in full regalia could be looked at only through smoked glass.

Baloo also accompanied us on camps. We went on a camp to
Heathcote, in the National Park. My mother came along to help. I
had talked her into coming by telling her that every other mother
would be there and that the campsite was yards from the station.
It was seven thousand yards from the station. Mine was the only
mother large-hearted enough to contribute her services. The trek
to the campsite was along bush tracks and down cliffs. Swinging
white-lipped from vines, my mother vowed to pick a bone with me
later. By the time we got to the campsite she was too far gone to
expend any of her remaining energy remonstrating with me. She
cooked the sausages while Akela and Baloo put up the tents. It took
Akela and Baloo about an hour's walk in the bush to find each tent
pole. Meanwhile my mother doled out the exploding sausages and
bandaged the hands of those Cubs – all of them heavily decorated

with badges denoting proficiency in woodcraft – who had burned
themselves picking up aluminium mugs of hot tea.

That night it rained like the Great Flood. The river rose. Tents
collapsed. All the Cubs ended up in one big tent with my mother.
Akela ended up in a pup tent with Baloo. Shortly afterwards they
were married. Presumably Akela gave birth to either a bear or a
wolf. By that time I had left the Cubs. You couldn't get into the
Scouts without a certain number of badges. My own score was
zero. Besides, I couldn't face a change of Akelas.

The big change I couldn't get out of was being sent to a special
school. In fourth class at Kogarah, when we were all about ten
years old, we took an IQ test. It was the Stanford–Binet, on which
I score about 140. On the more searching Wechsler–Bellevue I
get about 135. Such results are enough to put me into the 98th
percentile, meaning that 97 per cent of any given population is
likely to be less good at doing these tests than I am. This is nothing
to boast about. Intelligence starts being original only in the next
percentile up from mine, where the scores go zooming off the scale.
Time has taught me, too slowly alas, that there is nothing extraordinary about my mental capacities. In my romantic phase, which
lasted for too long, I was fond of blaming my sense of loneliness
on superior intellect. In fact the causes were, and are, psychological.

At the time, of course, none of these questions came up. My
mother was simply informed that her son had revealed himself
as belonging to a category which demanded two years of special
education in the Opportunity 'C' school at Hurstville. Opportunity
'A' schools were for the handicapped and Opportunity 'C' schools
were for the gifted. At either end of the scale special schooling
was a dubious privilege, since it involved travel by electric train.
Hurstville was only three stops down the Illawarra line but even
such a short voyage offered plenty of opportunities for sudden
death. Mothers very understandably worried themselves sick about
what their precious little sons might be getting up to on trains
that conveyed whole generations of schoolchildren at dizzy speeds
without benefit of automatic doors. For boys of any age it was

considered mandatory to stand near doorways. For older boys it was compulsory to stand at the very edge of the doorway, holding the door open with their shoulders, draping their arms negligently behind their backs with their hands loosely grasping the door handle, and keeping balance with their feet and legs as the swaying train hurtled through cuttings and over viaducts. Stanchions had been provided every hundred yards. They were meant to hold up the power lines, but had the additional function of braining anybody who stuck his head out of the window. Everybody stuck his head out of the window, drawing it back again as a stanchion loomed.

Every second train was a through, meaning it did not stop at Carlton and Allawah but attempted to break the world land-speed record on an uninterrupted run from Kogarah to Hurstville or vice versa. At either end it was considered de rigueur to alight as early as possible. Anyone waiting for the train to stop was considered a cissy. The more athletic boys could languidly step off and hit the platform running flat out. If they mistimed it they ended up with a gravel rash starting at the forehead and extending all the way to the toes. The sport came to an end when the champion, a boy named Newell, got his stations mixed up and stepped off at Allawah from the through train to Hurstville. When we got the news about his injuries – his left femur, apparently, was the only bone that remained intact – we became somewhat meeker about leaving the train early. Nevertheless the deaths continued to run at the rate of one a year. It was another ten years before automatic doors were tried out even experimentally. Perhaps someone was afraid that the Australian national character would be weakened.

At Hurstville there was an Opportunity 'C' fifth and sixth class with about thirty of us freaks in each class. Otherwise the school was normal. The freaks strove to be even more normal than everybody else – an instructive example of the Australian reluctance to stand out from the pack for any reason other than athletic skill. Some of our number, however, ranked as exotica no matter how hard they tried to blend into the scenery. There was a boy called

Nelson, for example, who made Graham Truscott look emaciated.
Nelson needed two desks. But he could play chess at an exalted
level. So could almost everybody else in the class except me. I
didn't even know the moves. A lot of the boys in the class wore
glasses and had notes from their parents excusing them from
soccer, swimming, running, jumping or even crossing the playground unattended. They were all drafted into the school's fife
band. On sports day they spent the afternoon marching awkwardly
backwards and forwards while playing 'Colonel Bogey' on their
black wooden fifes. The total effect was pathetic in the extreme.

The fife players also tended to wear those cissy sandals that
looked like ordinary shoes with bits cut out of them. Whenever I
could get away with it I defiantly stuck to bare feet. This was not,
I think, any kind of class-conscious social gesture. I had no inkling
of class differences. In Australia there is a widespread illusion that
there are no class barriers. In fact they exist, but it is possible to
remain unaware of them. There are social strata whose occupants
feel superior but there is almost nobody who feels inferior, probably because the poor are as well nourished as the rich. It never
occurred to me that most of the boys in the class came from more
privileged homes than mine. If I had been smarter it might have
done. The evidence was abundant. Graham Slender brought expensive toys to school. His father had bought them for him in America.
One of the toys was a machine gun that fired ping-pong balls. For
a few delirious seconds he showered the astonished class with
bouncing celluloid spheres before the gun was impounded. Robert
Lunn, David Carnaby, John Elstub and I usually occupied the back
four desks in the class. Lunn seemed inordinately well supplied
with funds. Sometimes after school he would shout half a dozen
of us to a cream-cake blow-out in one of the Hurstville tea shops.
He and I both knew what a blow-out was, since we had both
been reading English comics and boys' weeklies. Most Australian
boys at that time read American comics but a few read English
ones as well. With Lunn it was all in the family: his parents brought
him up in the English manner and eventually he went to Sydney

Grammar and after that to Duntroon. With me it was an accident.
When I had a suspected case of diphtheria just after the war I
was taken by screaming ambulance to South Coast Hospital near
Bunnerong powerhouse for three unforgettable weeks of ice cream
and lemonade. There were papers like *Tip-Top* and *Radio Fun* lying
around in the playroom. I made my mother buy more of them. On
visiting days my mother would arrive looking like a news vendor.
It took the edge off having to pee in a jar.

From then on I read *Tip-Top* every week and later graduated
to the *Wizard, Rover, Hotspur* and *Champion*. By the time I got to
Hurstville school I was an expert on these papers and could discuss
their contents endlessly. I certainly identified with characters like
Braddock VC and Alf Tupper, the Tough of the Track. Braddock
was a non-commissioned pilot who defeated the Luftwaffe single-
handed but contemptuously refused all promotions and decorations except the VC, whose ribbon he wore half hanging off.
Stuffed shirts were always objecting to his behaviour in railway
carriages and then having to apologize when they found out he was
the RAF's greatest hero. Alf Tupper trained on fish and chips and
ran the first four-minute mile. While admiring the prowess of these
demigods, I completely failed to realize that they were fantasy
figures specifically aimed at Britain's lower orders. Perhaps Lunn
had a better understanding but I suspect that he, too, was largely
in the dark. There was a serial in the *Wizard* about a poor lad
who with the aid of his tremendously self-sacrificing mother was
able to attend a public school. He wore patched trousers and had
to endure much scorn from the toffs but ended up Captain of
Swimming, Cricket, Football, Debates and finally of the School
itself. I don't think I really understood what this story was all
about. After all, in Australia all the schools were public – or so it
seemed. It never occurred to me that in an English context 'public'
meant 'private'. Possibly because I was clueless, but more likely
because the provocation simply wasn't there, I didn't develop any
kind of chip on my shoulder until much later, so the social content

of almost everything I was reading failed to register, even when social content was the only kind of content it had.

By this time I was starting to devour books as well as magazines and comics. I went Biggles-crazy and generally became an expert on aeroplanes. While the chess players were getting on with their chess I would be busy reading *Worrals Wipes It Off* or memorizing air-recognition charts. At the age of eleven I could recognize a photograph of any aircraft that had been built at any time in any country in the world. The Opportunity system gave its pupils plenty of time to develop such interests. The normal curriculum was dealt with in the morning and the afternoon was left free for the development of potentialities. Unfortunately like most educational concepts this idea yielded pretty thin results. No reflection on our teacher, Mr Davis – who had been a navigator in a Lancaster during the war and could turn a back somersault off the one-metre board – but learning to recognize aeroplanes is not the same as acquiring knowledge. The inevitable result was that those boys who were receiving some guidance from home flourished while those whose sole stimulus was the school did little more than fool around with 'projects'. Since the choice of project was left to us, the results were hopelessly variable as to quality. One boy with bifocals would be turning an old washing-machine into a particle accelerator while the boy at the next desk would be cutting out pictures of giraffes. I've just remembered the name of the boy at the next desk. His name was Tommy Pillans. He was unhappy at home and committed suicide in his first year with us – the first premature death in my generation. His desk was empty for only a few days. Then there was a reshuffle. Perhaps part of Nelson moved into it. Anyway, that was Tommy Pillans. Gone without a ripple. Not for the last time, I accommodated myself with ease to the idea of someone vanishing.

As well as glasses, John Elstub had all the other attributes of dampness – shoe-like sandals, knee-length khaki shorts, fife and a purse full of notes from his mother saying that he was not to be exposed to direct sunlight. The only day he ever appeared on

the soccer field he ran away from the ball. He was the son of an
academic of some kind and spent his time at home absorbing
the contents of the *Encyclopædia Britannica*. He always knew the
answers but had a way of calling out 'Sir! Sir!' that not even Sir
could stand. Elstub was a standing joke. Yet he was reading
Ulysses while I was learning to tell a Messerschmitt Bf. 109E from
a Bf. 109F. (The Bf. 109E had struts supporting the tailplane and
the Bf. 109F didn't.) I was invited to Elstub's house once. There
were a lot of pre-war American aviation magazines lying around.
I asked if I could borrow them and when I got home I cut them
up and pasted the best pictures in my scrapbooks. Next day at
school I presented Elstub with the fait accompli and he said it was
all right. It never occurred to me at the time that he had behaved
well and I badly, or that what I had done would have been
considered thoughtless in someone half my age. I was simply
convinced that aircraft were my department and that those magazines had no business being in Elstub's possession.

During the afternoons at school I spent a lot of time construct-
ing sandpit battlefields full of lead soldiers. Later on, copying the
school newspaper in *The Fifth Form at St Dominic's*, I started a wall
magazine to which everyone was invited to contribute. I usually
decided that hardly anybody's contributions were up to standard
except mine. At the annual exhibition day, held in the school
library, my sandpit battlefield made a huge impact. While all the
parents stood devoutly around, I explained the strategic picture
and announced that token detonations had been arranged in order
to represent the effect of artillery fire and tactical bombing. Actually
Slender, a dab hand at such matters, had sown the sand with
bungers which could be set off in sequence by touching a wire to a
battery. Slender was under the sand-tray with the battery. At the
rehearsal we used Kwong Man Lung penny bungers and everything
went all right. But for the performance proper Slender had planted
something more ambitious – fourpenny bungers the size of a stick
of dynamite. On top of this he got nervous and touched the whole
lot off at once. The Korean War was in progress at the time and

the parents must have thought that the Chinese communists had arrived in Hurstville. One man jumped into his wife's arms – an extraordinary role-reversal which I would have laughed at if I had not had a mouth full of sand. It was cowardly of Slender not to come out.

The wall magazine was rather better received. Verbally it was derivative in every respect, with stories about heroic wartime fliers, athletes training on fish and chips and stoic young school-boys rising above their patched trousers to become Captain of the School. Nearly all of it was written by me. But I shared responsibility for graphic design with David Carnaby. In the wall magazine, as in his notebooks, Carnaby had a subtle touch with lettering and a ravishing sense of colour. We usually shared the awards for the best set-out and decorated exercise books. I still like to think that my own lettering had a firmness of outline that his lacked. The grand designs were all mine. But he was unbeatable on tone and detail. Everything he did breathed a pastel elegance. It often happens that we are most touched by what we are least capable of. Evanescent delicacy is not the quality in the arts that I admire most, but it is often the characteristic by which I am most reduced to envy. Nowadays I know exactly what enchantment is being worked on me by Alain-Fournier's hedgerows or Monet's water lilies. I can put 'Miroirs' on the turntable and willingly succumb. I know that I can't do it myself but nowadays I can live with the knowledge. In those days I would look over Carnaby's shoulder and wonder if it was worth going on at all.

But go on I did, finding success easy. I was made class captain – a clear endorsement of my personality and attainments. There was thus no pressure on me to change my ways, which remained selfish, noisy and maladroit. At that time I was as big as, or bigger than, the boys around me, so it was not entirely absurd when I presumed to dominate them. As the teacher's representative I could usually make them toe the line, confident in the knowledge that it was less trouble for them to obey than to resist. My biggest coup was to maintain discipline through the long rehearsals for the

Queen's visit. This involved months of drill for every school in Sydney, so that finally when everything was put together in the Showground the Queen and Prince Philip would be stunned by a coordinated display of callisthenics and flag-waving. For two days before the actual event we shone our shoes, polished our belts, had our teeth filled, etc. On the day itself the school transferred en masse to the Showground, where our display team, with me as front right marker, lined up with hundreds of other such teams to await inspection by the Royal Party.

We stood for hours in the boiling sun. The Royal Party was running late. Children were fainting left and right, as if their serried ranks were subject to sniper fire. Suddenly there was a screech of tyres in the distance. The Queen and her consort screamed past us in a Land Rover. I remember that they were standing up. Each held on to the top of the windshield with one hand while giving the famous mechanical wave with the other. How their hats stayed on was a mystery, since they were travelling only slightly slower than a Formula One Grand Prix racing car. There were not too many details to remember, but it was evident that the Queen's complexion really was as advertised – peaches and cream. We then got on with our display. It was a measure of my almost psychopathic self-consciousness that I felt the Queen's eyes on me as I waved my flag. But I performed creditably, as did my team. Not counting Nelson, who had fainted long ago and been carried away on a couple of stretchers.

Generally it is our failures that civilize us. Triumph confirms us in our habits. I would probably have abused my power had I been given any. Fortunately my role as class captain was all responsibilities and no privileges. The most onerous duty was to keep order when Mr Davis was out of the room. I tried to do this by shouting 'Shut up!' at the top of my voice. Eventually I could stun the whole school by sheer lung-power. Otherwise, until the end of my stay there, Hurstville Opportunity 'C' hardly changed me at all, probably because what was going on at home was so intense.

I had enrolled myself in a family. The family were called the

Meldrums and lived in Sunbeam Avenue. Mr Meldrum was a plumber. He and Mrs Meldrum had produced three children, all boys: in descending order of age they were Gary, Neil and Craig. There was also an Alsatian dog called Ruth, whom I will get to in a minute. All six of them lived in a house not much bigger than ours. Mr Meldrum wore a blue working singlet at all times. He was regarded in the district as something of a gypsy. In fact he was simply the most original man for miles. He made hardly any money but there was more going on in his house than in anybody else's. He had turned all the boys into good swimmers. Gary was exceptionally good and got his picture in the papers for swimming a mile at the age of ten. Neil was a bit of a black sheep and Craig was simply dense, but even they were encouraged in their interests. Neil was mad about stamps and Craig was held by Mr Meldrum to be a promising biologist. In fact Craig's biological studies consisted mainly of picking up privet grubs and eating them. He would also tuck into the occasional centipede. Mrs Meldrum's understandable hysteria at such moments would be overwhelmed by Mr Meldrum's gusto. He was the first man I ever met who had that. In short, he was a ready-made father figure.

The Meldrums taught me to swim. Mr Meldrum, Gary and Neil took me down to the creek in the park. Reeds lined the banks and willows kissed the surface. The water was as brown as oxtail soup but Mr Meldrum said that any water was clean if you could catch healthy fish in it. All the Meldrums could swim across the creek underwater. To me it seemed a fabulous distance. Gary showed me how to hold my breath and keep my eyes open underwater. I could see his hair floating. Inside an hour I was dog-paddling. Mr Meldrum threw his own boys up in the air to turn back somersaults. Then I rode on Gary's shoulders, Neil rode on his father's, and we had battles in the shallow water.

That was just the start. I think I was eight years old, or perhaps nine. Over the next few years I spent more and more time at the Meldrums'. I would bolt my dinner and scoot around to their place in time to join them for a second dessert. Thus I laid the foundation of my uncanny ability to inhale a meal instead of eating it. Another bad aspect was the inevitable encounter with Ruth. Like all dog-owning families, the Meldrums regarded their four-footed friend as some kind of genius. Ruth was Mr Meldrum's blind spot. He seemed to think that his house would not be safe without Ruth to guard it. Apart from an abundance of life there was nothing in the house worth stealing. Nor, had there been, would Ruth have ranked as an early choice to stand sentinel. She was undoubtedly ferocious enough, but was no brighter than any other dog. She vented most of her fury on the family and its close acquaintances. If any burglars had turned up she would probably have ignored them, or else let them in and minded their tools. For me, on the other hand, she never failed to go through her entire repertoire of savagery. While I waited, yelling weakly, on the outside of the trellis gate in the side passage, Ruth would hurl herself against the inside of it like a piledriver and try to bite a piece out of it big enough to get at me through. I would stand petrified until a few of the Meldrums turned up, clubbed their pet into submission and dragged it back out of sight. Upon receipt of a written, signed guarantee that Ruth had been stapled to the ground with croquet hoops, I would advance trembling and join the family for dessert, tea and games.

There were scraps of dog-meat on the floor of the back veranda but Mr Meldrum's Rabelaisian spirit turned the chaos and squalor into luxury. He was a great one for word games after dinner. As a natural diplomat he was able to cope with the fact that I often turned out to be better at these than his own sons. Seeking his favour, I was too keen ever to try less hard. When the word games were over Mr and Mrs Meldrum would listen to the wireless in the lounge while the rest of us would try to cross the spare room in the dark without getting caught by the guard. You took turns being guard. The spare room lay at the end of the corridor and I remember it as being the size of the Grand Salon in the Louvre, although I suppose it could have been no bigger than a box room. Old cupboards and other articles of furniture were stored in it. It could be blacked out perfectly, so crossing it undetected was a test of the ability to move silently while consumed with fear. Neil had a scary trick, when he was guard, of dressing up in some frightening costume and suddenly switching the light on. The mere possibility of his doing this was enough to make the hair rise on my neck the way it did at the pictures when the music indicated tension or impending doom.

On Saturday afternoons Mr Meldrum led expeditions to the Domain. The Domain, or Dom, was an old swimming baths opposite Woolloomooloo on the south side of Sydney Harbour. We got off the train at St James and walked to the baths through long lanes of Moreton Bay fig trees. At the Dom we changed into blue vees and swam. The benches on the bleached wooden cat-walks of the Dom were weighed down with ancient wrecks soaking up the sun. Men older than John D. Rockefeller or Pope Pius XIII shuffled dazedly around, their vees draped approximately across their shrivelled loins, their skins burned so brown that their sprinklings of black skin cancers looked like currants in a fruit-cake. But the main point was that they had lived a long time. Mr Meldrum was obviously right about the preservative effects of sea water.

Mr Meldrum, Gary, Neil and Craig always did well in the swimming races. To me it seemed too much like hard work. I had some of the knack for swimming but I lacked the will. My main reason for going to the Dom with the Meldrums was to be able to go home with them afterwards. On the way back through the trees to St James station Mr Meldrum bought huge paper bags full of fruit. We gorged ourselves on grapes and plums and had battles with the Moreton Bay figs lying around in thousands on the grass. On the train there were more word games. Laved and cured by salt water, fed to repletion with unadulterated fruit, we were in a state of grace.

For the rest of the weekend Gary was the ringleader. While Mr Meldrum was off doing the extra jobs which were obviously all that kept the bailiffs from the door, Gary was the one who led the

great treks to Botany Bay or the dump at Tempe. Down at the
bay in the early winter mornings we used to watch the fishermen
pull in the nets and were usually given a few yellowtail or bream to
take home. Before they built the refinery at Kurnell the bay used
to be as full of fish as when Banks and Solander first stepped
ashore. At Tempe dump I uncovered choice items for what was to
become one of the world's leading collections of old piston rings,
rusty egg-beaters, quondam bed-springs and discarded trans-
mission components for Sherman tanks. I shall not attempt to
describe my mother's joy when I lugged this stuff home, staggering
out of the sunset long after she had called the police. A dump in
those days, before plastics had conquered the world, was a treasury
of precious metals.

It was Gary who led the first, historic expedition to Kingsford
Smith aerodrome, always known to us by the name of the suburb
near where it was situated, Mascot. The aerodrome was only a few
miles distant – in fact our house was quite near the first set of
approach lights to the main runway – but walking all the way there
and back seemed a feat comparable in daring to anything con-
templated by Burke and Wills. As for Mascot itself, it was simply
fairyland. Until well along in my teens I went there almost every
weekend, just to watch the aircraft land and take off. ANA and
TAA were flying mainly DC-3s and DC-4s. The arrival of the first
DC-6 was a big event. The first Stratocruiser flight to arrive from
America was greeted with national rejoicing. The TAA ground staff
let us take a look inside a Convair 240. Gary found the *Southern
Cross* standing in a hangar with its tyres down. I suppose after
Smithy's last flight they just wheeled it in there and left it. Standing with her nose tilted snootily upward in the gloom, the old blue
Fokker tri-motor looked romantic past belief. There was no one in
there with her except us. Gary couldn't get the cabin door open.
But on a nearby stretch of waste ground there was the wingless hull
of an amphibian Catalina. The guns had been taken out but the
turrets and blisters were still in her. We used to climb inside and
play wars for hours. Gary and I were pilot and navigator. Neil had

the nose turret and Craig was the waist gunner – a good position for him, since among the ribs and stringers there were plenty of spiders to be caught and eaten. Defending Mascot from Japanese and German attack, we shot down hundreds of Zeros and FW-190s.

The Meldrums' back veranda was a combination of dormitory, playroom and workshop. All three of the boys had their beds there. Each bed had its own set of shelves for a headboard. Neil's shelves held his stamp albums and catalogues. Craig's were a teeming, pulsing nightmare of chicken embryos and legless frogs. Gary's shelves were full of balsa model aircraft made from kits. Solid balsa kits are unheard-of nowadays, when all the skill required to make a model aircraft is a light touch with the plastic parts and a steady hand with the glue. In those days you matched a block of balsa against a rudimentary diagram and got going with a razor blade, which sliced your thumb as readily as it carved the balsa. If the result was recognizable as an aeroplane, you were an expert. If your thumb was recognizable as a thumb, you were a genius. Gary worked fast and accurately. He built a Ju.88, a Hawker Sea Fury, a Heinkel He.III, a Kitty Hawk, a Chance-Vought Corsair . . . I can remember them all. He would have had an air force if he had looked after them. But when he got tired of having them around he soaked them with dope and set fire to them. The glue came in a tube and was called Tarzan's Grip. If I close my eyes I can remember how it felt to squeeze the last tiny transparent blob from the malleable lead tube.

7. EROS AND THE ANGEL

It was love, of course. Gary was older than I was, sure of himself, capable at everything he tackled. I suppose my sexuality would have awoken by itself but he was certainly in on the beginning of it, although by the time I was getting passionate about him he was getting passionate about girls. Having already started masturbating without knowing even vaguely what I was at, I was delighted to discover that someone else did it and even got visible results. While I was still coming nothing but air Gary was able to conjure a whole vichyssoise into being. It probably never occurred to him that our mutual masturbation sessions were looked forward to by me, and looked back on afterwards, with a romantic, jealous fervour that could keep me awake for hours. Neil did his best to keep us apart out of what seemed to me sheer spite. I grew to hate Neil.

I don't think Gary was in any way homosexual or even bisexual. He was just bung full of juice, and attracted by the idea of initiating me in the ways of sex, which he was able to find out about at a precocious rate, since girls found him very attractive. After a day of battles with willow bows and reed arrows in the bush and swamp on the far side of the park, Gary would be the one who spotted the pairs of lovers parking their cars and heading for the ferns, wherein they would disappear by the simple expedient of lying down. Gary was the one who had a name for what they were up to. Neil was the one who made the mistake of firing an arrow. Reed arrows were dry, brittle and weightless until we tipped them with a piece of copper wire driven into the capillary left by the missing pith. Having no tail, the arrows lacked accuracy, but they could go a surprisingly long way if the bow was any good. Neil had spent a long time selecting his bow. It was strung so taut that it played a note when he plucked it. We were observing a distant area of ferns into which a courting couple had vanished some time before. In a low voice, Gary was imparting the unbelievable information that they were playing with each other in order to have babies. It was a fascinating speech until interrupted by a soft twang.

It would have been bad enough if the man had stood up with one hand holding the arrow and the other holding his behind. Unfortunately it was the woman. The man was running towards us, buckling his belt. We lost him by ducking into the swamp. Even then Neil's insane giggle might well have given us away. Apart from Kenny Mears, Neil was the first example I ever encountered of someone who lacked any idea of a given action having necessary consequences. If he felt like hitting you with an axe, he hit you with an axe. Once Gary and I built a tepee in the backyard. Craig sat inside it pretending to be an Indian, an impression he reinforced by preparing himself a light snack of worms and woodlice. The rest of us danced around the tent pretending to be other Indians attacking. Neil had a garden stake for a spear. He hurled it full force at the tent. Craig came screaming out of the tent with the garden stake sticking straight out of his kidneys. It often happened that way. Neil would have a brainwave and shortly afterwards you would hear the sirens.

My erection-consciousness was exacerbated by Gary, who harped on the words 'big' and 'fat' until they became automatically funny. Whenever anybody used either of these words in conversation, Gary would smile at me and I would snicker uncontrollably. Similarly uncontrollable was my virile organ, which chose the most inconvenient moments to expand. For some reason riding on the top deck of the trolleybus led to a spontaneous show of strength. On the lower deck it didn't happen. I rode on the lower deck whenever possible, but sometimes I was forced upstairs, where my short trousers had a lot to cope with from the moment I sat down. Placed casually across my lap and held down with one negligent arm, my Globite school case kept things covered until we got to

Kogarah station, but getting off the bus was a problem. If the bus terminated at Kogarah I could wait until everybody else had alighted, but if it was going on to Rockdale then I had to disembark come what might. There was a choice of carrying my school case unnaturally in front of me or else hopping along doubled over. At school there was the desk to hide under. As far as I could tell, nobody else at Hurstville had the same problem. It wasn't until I got to high school that cock-consciousness spread to fill the whole day.

At school there were friendships and crushes, but nothing physical except the usual business of walking around arm in arm. At home there was rampant sexuality, most of it centred on Gary. But if I was queer for him, it was the outward expression of an inward yearning for the feminine. My dreams were all of girls, even if I didn't, at that stage, connect what I dreamed of doing to them – I remember fantasies of being pressed against them very tightly – with what I actually did in Gary's company. Not long after the war, when I was just starting at Kogarah Primary, my mother took me for a week's holiday at Katoomba. The hotel was called the Sans Souci – the same name, confusingly, as a suburb just near Kogarah, on the George's River. But Katoomba was a long way away, in the Blue Mountains, surrounded by famous tourist attractions like the Scenic Railway, the Three Sisters, the Everglades gardens at Leura and the Jenolan caves. Another husbandless mother staying at the hotel had a daughter my age who wore lace dresses. I christened her Lacy Skirts, after Gary's best guinea pig.

Lacy Skirts was my first case of the *visione amorosa*. I lurked for hours near her staircase just to get a glimpse of her. Somehow I managed to get to know her and we played chasings around the hotel. Rarely touching her, I had such an awareness of her physical existence that my chest hurt every time I looked at her. I never spoke of my feelings and so never found out what she felt for me, but I can remember clearly (probably because the vision was to keep recurring, each time with a different object, for many years to come) that my obsession was as transforming and exalting as whatever passed through the heart of Augustine Meaulnes in the brief time he spent with Yvonne de Galais. A picture of Lacy Skirts is no longer in my head, but my adoration for her is still the central memory of that holiday – a fair measure of intensity, since a lot else happened. I got earache on the bus to Jenolan as it wound around the mountains. Touring the limestone caves, I was in frightful pain, and was already crying when I ran off into the bush to pee. Running back to the bus again, I tripped over in full sight of everybody and fell into a patch of giant stinging nettles. Pelion was piled on Ossa. Happening one on top of the other, the earache and the nettles constituted an almost biblical attack on one's equilibrium. Job wouldn't have stood for it. But concentrate as I might, I can't recall the pain, whereas when I think of Lacy Skirts, even though I can't bring back her face, I can recall exactly the sensation of beatitude. We forget the shape of the light but remain dazzled for ever.

My next amorous vision was the Pocket Venus. Again we were on holiday, this time at a resort on the Hawkesbury River called Una Voce, which was pronounced Ewna Vose even by its proprietors. Being by then almost eleven years old, I was better able to stay out of my mother's hair. If there were any patches of giant nettles, I managed to walk around them, instead of falling in. It was my mother who gave my vision its name. We were having lunch in the dining room on our first day in residence when a small adolescent girl walked in. She had on a soft pale pink blouse, white shorts and gold sandals laced up the calf, in the manner of a miniaturized, tennis-playing Greek goddess. Sitting there in my short trousers with my feet nowhere near touching the floor, I instantly realized that my lack of years was an irreversible tragedy. There seemed no hope of making her aware that I was alive. I lurked in the corridors waiting for an opportunity to walk suddenly past her. There was, of course, no question of actually addressing her in words. As I remember it, my plan was to attract her attention by the intensity of my walk. The idea was to look so lost in thought that she would be unable to resist asking what the thought was.

Alas, she resisted successfully for days on end, despite the fact that she was unable to travel far in any direction without having her path abruptly crossed by a short, swiftly moving philosopher.

When I wasn't hanging around the corridors I was immersed in the swimming pool, waiting for her to appear so that she could be impressed by my ability to swim across and back underwater. Since the pool was no bigger than a sheep dip this was scarcely a great feat, but with the exception of the Pocket Venus everyone sitting around the pool was ready to agree, when prompted, that I had the amphibian properties of a platypus. The Pocket Venus was never there to agree about anything. On the day she finally showed up, she was wearing a light blue satin one-piece costume and looked more beautiful than the mind could bear. Desperate for recognition, I took a deep breath and went into my act. The stress of the moment, however, caused me to take this deep breath under the surface instead of above it. Having travelled about a yard, I emerged with my hair in my eyes and my lungs full of water. Exercising heroic self-control, I did not cough or splutter, but managed a terrible half smile which was meant to indicate that I had just thought of something important enough to warrant interrupting an otherwise inevitably successful assault on the world swimming record. When my vision cleared, the Pocket Venus was no longer there. She had changed her mind and gone back up to the guest house. Such moments should have been educational but unfortunately there is nothing to indicate that self-consciousness can be lessened by proof of the world's indifference.

Every night there was a social in the ballroom. Wallflower was an insufficient word to describe me. I was a wallshadow, a wallstain. In order to conceal my short trousers I stood behind things. Boys only a few years older than I were dancing with her – actually *touching* her. But those few years were an unbridgeable chasm. On the far side of the abyss lay long trousers, an Adam's apple, depth of voice and tallness of stature. On the near side lay bare knees, a piping treble, sweaty hands and a head that stuck out at the back. For months that grew into years I was to spend a good part of every day checking my profile with two mirrors, hoping to find my chin sticking out more and the back of my head sticking out less. I envied boys with no backs to their heads. Even today I envy James Garner. At all costs I had to minimize the number of occasions on which the Pocket Venus could see my head from the side. I modified my approach in the corridors so that my head was always pointing straight at her even when my body was in profile. I was lucky not to walk out of a window, instead of merely into a waiter carrying a tray of custards and junkets. Even then she didn't notice me.

She finally noticed me on the second last day of the holiday. It was in the ping-pong room – a context in which noticing me was hard to avoid, since I had developed a style of play so elaborately baroque that I must have looked like one of those Russian girl gymnasts who dance with a ribbon. Every stroke of the bat was counterbalanced with an upflung pose from the other hand. The general effect, I later realized, must have been more comic than impressive: mere virtuosity, however precocious, could not have attracted such crowds. On the other hand it was impossible to imagine the Pocket Venus being cruel. It must have been kindness that led her to pick up a bat and ask if she could play. She was bad enough at it to make us an even match. We played half that day and all the next morning. I talked endlessly, trying to fascinate her. At least twenty years were to go by before I began realizing that there is no point in such efforts – what women like about us is seldom something we are conscious of and anyway people don't want to be charmed, they want to charm. I probably couldn't have managed things worse, but for a wonder she seemed to like my company, despite my never falling silent except when we touched (it was permissible to brush against her slightly when changing ends) or when she bent over to pick up the ball. When she did that I caught such glimpses of the lace edges of her panties under her shorts that I was drained of all motion. Suddenly I was a dead mackerel. She would straighten up with the ball in her hand and find herself confronted with someone who looked as if he had been zapped with a death ray or injected with cement.

Reality dispelled the dream only to the extent of revealing my light of love to be a nice, ordinary girl. I fell more in love than ever and could hardly breathe for grief when the boat took me and my mother away and left the Pocket Venus behind. The Hawkesbury had flooded during our stay and was by then almost up to the front porch of the guest house, so she was only a few feet away from me as we waved goodbye. Dropping away on the fast-flowing muddy current – the whole flux dotted thickly for miles with countless oranges from the ruined orchards – I looked back on her as she grew smaller, already embarked on the rearward voyage that would take the details of her inexpressibly sweet face beyond the reach of my memory.

No, there was never any real question about which sex I would love when the time came. But not for years would the time come, and in the meanwhile I was as queer as a coot. For most of my two-year stretch at Hurstville I led a double life. At home there were vividly physical encounters with Gary, involving a good deal of mutual masturbation, which must have been a lot more inter-esting for me than for him, since he had something you could get a grip on, and which produced tangible results. At school I formed crushes on the other boys. In an English public school such passionate attachments would presumably have led to buggery, rape, torture and perhaps death, but in a Sydney day school there was not much that could happen. Nevertheless the emotions were real, although it was often embarrassing to discover that they were not reciprocated in equal strength, or indeed at all. I was far keener on walking with my arm around Carnaby, for example, than he was on walking with his arm around me. But at least he took me home to show me his Dinky Toys, of which he had an amazing collection. There were avowals of inseparable companionship. I did the avowing and he nodded, or at any rate didn't shake his head.

Other boys in the class might have been more forthcoming but I was interested only in the optimates. In my fancy, we were a band of brothers – the Boys in the Back Desks. On the last day of school our class, 6A1, had to provide two teams for a softball tournament against the regular sixth class, called 6A. There was a first team and a second team. Despite my position as class captain, I somehow ended up in the second team along with all the duds in weird sandals, while the optimates headed off together over the horizon, never to be seen again as a group. I was so disappointed I couldn't even cry. For days afterwards I turned the disaster over and over in my mind, trying to think of how I might have managed things differently. I even told my mother about it. Her advice was to forget it, since the day would come when I would look back on it and laugh. She was only half right. The day eventually came when I could look back on it without howling in anguish, but closer to equanimity than that I never came. Far bigger things have gone wrong for me since, but nothing has ever seemed so unfair. I can see why it hurt then. What is hard to see is why it should still hurt now.

Behind this apparent disaster lay a real disaster, unappreciated by me at the time. My marks had won me a bursary to Sydney Boys' High School. If I had gone there I might have been educated in some of the ways of a gentleman. I suppose that was not much of a loss. More to be regretted was that I might have been educated in some of the ways of Latin, Greek, English literature, or indeed anything. That Sydney High School counted as one of the so-called Great Public Schools was a side issue. The central point to notice was that its academic standards were unquestionable. The same could not be said of Sydney Technical High School. Unlike Sydney High, which was well situated near Moore Park, Sydney Tech was a tumbledown collection of old buildings in Paddington, a district which was still fifteen years from being rediscovered by the conservationists, and which was at that time still largely inhabited by prostitutes too jaded for the brighter lights around the docks. Nor was it GPS. Instead it was CHS, or Combined High Schools – a difference its representatives spent a lot of time saying didn't matter. Nor would it have mattered, if Sydney Tech had truly been able to claim any special distinction. As it was, however, those parents who sent their boys there under the impression that they would receive outstanding instruction in mathematics and the sciences were being hoodwinked. Sydney Tech might have been a good school before my time there. For all I know it has been a good school again since I left. But while I was in attendance it was mediocre at best.

But my wanting to go there wasn't the place's fault – apart, that is, from the fact that Carnaby was on the way there too. Elstub was bound for Sydney High, naturally enough: he knew what he wanted and his father knew that that was the best place to get it. Lunn was bound for Sydney Grammar – another suitable choice. Carnaby had a marked gift for mathematics, so Sydney Tech made some kind of sense for him. But it made no sense for me to choose Sydney Tech just because Carnaby was going there. As so often happens, however, the irrational motives were the decisive ones. The rational motive – that I thought I wanted to be an aeronautical engineer – I could have been talked out of if it had been properly explained to me that Sydney High produced more of those than Sydney Tech did. But the urge to follow Carnaby was proof even against my mother's distress, which was understandably torrential. The news that Sydney Tech had a squadron of air cadets put the matter beyond question, as far as I was concerned. I imagined myself at the controls of a Mustang taking off from the school playground.

My mother wanted me to have all the prestige that Sydney High would undoubtedly bring. She didn't want to have to go around hoarsely insisting that Sydney Tech was really something rather marvellous. With Sydney High there was nothing to insist about. Everyone knew that Sydney High was as good as you could get. And Sydney High, which people fought to get their sons into, had asked me to enrol! How could I not? She didn't get it. For months she kept on and for months I fought back. She was right, of course, but it didn't help. I owed it to her as a reward for all her work. It would have been better if I had given in. It would have been better still if the means had existed to make me do the right thing no matter how determined I was on doing the wrong. But on her own she was no match for me. I just wore her down.

8. THE IMITATION OF CHRIST

Thus, by a long battle of attrition, the matter was decided. But the beginning of my first year at Sydney Tech was still a long way away, at the far end of the school holidays. By this time the Meldrum boys had become regular attendants at Kogarah Presbyterian Church, which was situated about halfway between Prince's Highway and the station. Mr Meldrum, a rationalist, would have disapproved of this development. Unfortunately Mr Meldrum was no longer around. A load of pipes had slid off his flat-bed truck and pinned him to a wall. He was brought home to die. The process took several weeks. By now a seasoned campaigner, I had prudently withheld from him the vital last tenth of my affection, so I was well able to survive the shock: indeed I hardly noticed it, since by some inexplicable coincidence I took to calling at the Meldrum house with steadily decreasing frequency. Others, notably Mrs Meldrum, were less well armoured against fortune. She was prostrated. Not just to get some relief from their presence, but also to prepare them against an uncertain world, she started sending her boys to church. After a decent interval I followed.

Kogarah Presbyterian Church was a solid purple-brick and red-tile affair with plaster interiors. Standing opposite the St George District Hospital, it was handily placed to entertain the polio patients with massed singing of 'Onward, Christian Soldiers'. Many a surgeon must have paused gratefully during a tricky operation to relish the top notes of our resident coloratura, Mrs Pike, as she howled above the choir like a dingo with its paw caught in a trap. Scalpels must have frozen in mid-slice as the Boys' Brigade bugle band came marching by, emitting a rich collection of wrong notes and raspberries. One way and another the whole of Sunday and half the rest of the week saw the wee kirk teeming with activity. It was a whole way of life. I plunged into it gladly, egged on by my mother. I was supposed to be Church of England, but she wouldn't have minded if I had been going to a mosque, as long as I went.

My previous Christian experience had been confined to an interdenominational Sunday School run by the Purvis family at their house halfway down Sunbeam Avenue. Mrs Purvis played the piano and Mr Purvis showed 16mm films of aborigines being converted. In the early part of the film the aborigines were shown standing around naked with a crotch full of shadows and looking glum while flies camped on their faces. In the later part of the film they were wearing trousers and smiling like Loretta Young. It was Christ who had made the difference. They had taken Him into their hearts, whereupon the flies had upped stakes and moved on. When the lights went up Mr Purvis would launch into an attack on beer and Catholicism. He pronounced beer bee-ar. The legionaries who pee-arsed Christ's side with a spee-ar had undoubtedly been enslaved to bee-ar. A sure sign of Catholicism's fundamental evil was that it required the drinking of wine even in church, wine being mee-arly another form of bee-ar. Mr Purvis would then get us to sign the pledge all over again and send us home with a warning not to be kidnapped by nuns.

But the Purvises' Sunday School was strictly short pants, striped T-shirt and bare feet. We would have grown out of it anyway, even if Mrs Purvis hadn't died of cancer. The piano having fallen silent, there was nothing for Mr Purvis to do except remarry, move to Melbourne and start again. He became famous years later as an anti-Catholic campaigner, warning of attempts by the Vatican to invade Canberra. Once again he had films to prove it. Nuns were shown scurrying darkly down side streets, while a familiar voice on the soundtrack talked of how the Roman menace loomed ever more nee-ar, and of the growing fee-ar that it would soon be hee-ar.

Kogarah Presbyterian Church was the big time. On Sunday morning there was Sunday School, followed by church, at which the Boys' Brigade would frequently put in an appearance with snare drums rattling in approximate unison and dented bugles giving out random fragments of late Schönberg. In the early evening there would be church. Then there was a Fellowship meeting for older adolescents and young adults. This would be followed by church again, featuring a full-scale sermon from the Reverend C. Cummings Campbell, whose name was the inspiration of many a leaden joke ('the Campbells are Cummingses, yes they are,' etc.) and whose oratory bored the pigeons out of the roof. If you threw in and averaged out all the Harvest Festivals, preparations for Harvest Festivals, special study sessions for Sunday School teachers, special missionary group studies for Fellowship Study Circle leaders and so on, it would be possible to say that the devout young communicant could count on spending most of each week in constant attendance, with the odd break for meals. On Saturday night there was usually a Fellowship social. On Thursday night the Boys' Brigade drilled in the church hall. At one time or another, as I grew older, I took part in all these activities, starting with Sunday School and the Boys' Brigade.

Sunday School was a waste of time from the religious angle, but had conspicuous social value. A hundred children broken up into ten groups of ten, we learned the fundamental disciplines of sitting still for an hour while an older person told boring stories. Apart from the chance to take home a deckle-edged sticker, stick it in a book and bring the book back to be marked, there was no action. The stickers had luridly coloured biblical illustrations on them. There was also a catechism to be learned. Prizes were to be won for learning it. Thus the memory was tested, if not the religious sense. Over the next five or six years I won every possible prize, up to and including the rarely awarded Cummings Campbell Bible, without experiencing, or even needing to pretend I had experienced, a moment of religious belief. Among the teachers, the few genuine believers were manifestly as crazy as Mr Purvis. Any sign of true devotion among the pupils was regarded as bad taste. Eventually I was to become a teacher myself and make a practice of getting the holy stuff over as soon as possible so that I could get on with telling stories about Pearl Harbor or the campaign in the Western Desert. No pupil ever complained.

But that's to jump the gun. As a new Sunday School pupil I learned how to sit still with girls present. As a probationary recruit in the Boys' Brigade I learned how to march up and down. The Boys' Brigade was a paramilitary organization emanating, like the Scouts, from England, but with the emphasis on parade-ground drill rather than on woodsy lore. The uniform had to be imported from England. It consisted of forage cap, white cartridge pouch and brass-buckled belt, the whole thing worn over khaki shorts and navy blue shirts, although in winter we were expected to wear dark suits. One of the main attractions of belonging was that the merit badges, worn on the right sleeve, were made of what looked like solid silver. In practice these tended not to arrive from England even after repeated notifications that they had been won, but you could always live in hope. Another main attraction was that you got the chance to blow a bugle or bang a drum. It was with high expectations, therefore, that I set off for my first evening on parade.

My manner of dress perhaps showed questionable judgement. As a new recruit I was not entitled to wear Boys' Brigade uniform even if it had been available. To compensate I eked out my shorts, shirt and sandshoes with a few extras. On my head I put one of Ray's old RAAF forage caps with its flaps down. The cap was covered with about a hundred badges of various kinds, many of them celebrating our recent alliance with the Soviet Union. There were several portraits of Stalin. On my chest I wore my father's campaign medals – not just the ribbons, but the medals entire. Usually I was allowed to wear these only on Anzac Day when we went into town to watch the march, but my mother had given me a special dispensation. On my belt was a holster containing a Ned Kelly cap pistol fully loaded. A multi-purpose jack-knife completed the ensemble. Since I was still quite small the jack-knife weighed me down on one side. I thought better of it and took it off. My mother persuaded me that the medals were perhaps gilding the lily, so I took those off too. The rest I kept.

Kindly Captain Andrews, the senior officer, forbore from comment on my appearance. There wasn't much he noticed by that stage. Having grown old in the task, he tended to daydream. I fell in at the low end of a long line, which then divided itself into four sections of half a dozen boys each. Everyone started off as a private. The mere ability to turn up once a week ensured one's eventual promotion to lance corporal. If your voice broke it was enough to make you a full corporal. To become a sergeant you had to pass a few exams. Beyond that lay the dizzy privilege of officer status, featuring long trousers and a cap with ribbons hanging down at the back. Down at my end of the scale it all looked very impressive, but even while occupying a rank more lowly than private I could see that Captain Andrews wasn't too hot at drill. When he said 'About turn!' we about-turned. When he said 'About turn!' again we about-turned again. He then showed us how we should have done it. Facing towards us, he ordered himself to about-turn. By rights, upon completion of this manoeuvre, he should have been facing away from us, so that we could see his back. Instead he would end up facing sideways, so that we could see him in profile. Quickly he would add a few shuffles to take him round the rest of the way. Gary was the corporal at the head of my section. I could see his shoulders quaking every time Captain Andrews got it wrong. That got me started. Thus a sense of the ridiculous was inculcated, at an early age. For years to come I found almost everyone ludicrous except myself.

In fact the Kogarah Presbyterian Church Company of the Boys' Brigade was a shambles. Annually we came last in the district drill competition, even when it was held in our own hall. Our bugle band terrorized not just the hospital but the whole area, with bitches whelping at its strident dissonance. Not long after I joined there was a Display Night, held in conjunction with Girls' Brigade. My mother was horrified to discover that her tiny son was last in a line of crouching small boys over which, or whom, large girls awkwardly dived before turning a forward roll on a mat. Her fears were justified. Graham Truscott's older sister Maureen was built

like Fatty Arbuckle and looked no lovelier for being clad in black
sandshoes, blue shorts and a singlet like a two-car garage. As proud
parents sat open-mouthed on the surrounding benches, she came
hurtling out of the back annexe, along the corridor, through the
connecting door, into the hall, up to the springboard and into
space. She drove me into the floor like a tack. Artificial respiration
got my breathing started while Captain Andrews and the Rev. C.
Cummings Campbell attempted to calm my mother with a few
ill-chosen words.

Such incidents were too common to be thought remarkable. At
the District Athletics Carnival held at Trumper Park our company
got no points. Count them: none. In the swimming carnivals
Gary was our only swimmer ever to reach the finals of anything.
As part compensation there was a great deal of rod-walloping. Masturbation, whether solo, mutual or of competition standard, was
rife. So was petty theft. After a hard evening of copying Captain
Andrews's about-turns we would all race down to Parry's milk
bar, there to ingest the milkshake of our choice and rob the lolly
counter when Mr Parry wasn't looking. The only time Mr Parry
ever caught one of us he contented himself with delivering a white-
lipped lecture. It was a wonder he didn't call the police. Anywhere
in the world, immigrant shopkeepers have a particular horror of
being robbed by the locals. It hurts to work so hard and suddenly
discover that some of your customers subscribe to Proudhon's idea
about property being theft. If Proudhon had been running the milk
bar he would probably have reacted far worse than Mr Parry.
Luckily for us, Proudhon had been dead since 1865.

The other half of my double life had more hesitant beginnings.
It wasn't that I hated Sydney Tech. I just didn't connect with it.
On weekday mornings I put on my school uniform. It consisted,
reading from bottom to top, of black shoes, grey socks, grey
worsted short-pants suit with school pocket badge, blue shirt, tie in
the school colours of maroon and sky blue and grey felt hat with
hat band in school colours. Add in the enamel school lapel badge
and you had an awful lot of maroon and sky blue. Exercise books,

pencil case, pens, technical-drawing set and Vegemite sandwiches went into the inevitable Globite school case. Lugging this, I rode the trolleybus to Kogarah station and caught the train to Central. Other Sydney Tech boys were already on the train from stations further down the line. As we got closer to town, more joined. Boys from Sydney High also got on. Their colours were chocolate and sky blue. Age for age, they seemed slightly taller than our lot, with clearer skins. They were quieter and read a great deal. At Central they caught one tram while we caught another. They went to Moore Park and we went to Paddington. Nobody except a few aesthetes had any idea at the time that Paddington's terrace houses were desirable residences. Gentrification lay far in the future. The only paint on show was kack brown and the cast-iron balconies looked like scrap metal waiting to be taken away. It wasn't a slum area like Redfern – which during the Queen's visit had been masked off with hessian so that she would be unable to see it from the royal train – but it was pretty grim. Sydney Tech was in the grimmest part and looked even grimmer than its surroundings. The playgrounds were entirely asphalt: not a blade of grass. A solitary Moreton Bay fig tree in the lower playground was the only touch of green. Jammed between the dilapidated two-storey buildings, even less prepossessing 'temporary' single-storey buildings cut the playground space down to nearly nothing. In the open air there wasn't enough bench space for the whole school to sit down at once. We had to have lunch in two shifts.

Disaster struck on the first day, when Carnaby was assigned to a different class. In quiet desperation I sought out his company in the playground, but often he lunched in the other shift and always he was surrounded by new friends. So it had all been for nothing.

I didn't even get accepted for the Air Cadets. The fact that I knew more about air recognition than anyone else in the world counted as nothing beside the further fact that I had an unacceptable level of albumin in my blood. An independent pathologist wrote a note saying that my level of albumin was all right for me but the RAAF doctor wouldn't listen. If such an injustice had happened to me earlier it might have helped arm me against capricious Fate, but I was too spoiled to profit from the disappointment. Many, many years were to go by before I learned the truth of Noël Coward's comment about the secret of success being the capacity to survive failure.

Soon enough I made new friends in my own class, but not in the same way as Carnaby did. His natural authority was reinforced by early maturity. Either that year or the year after, his voice broke. He had acne for about two days and simultaneously grew a foot taller. During this period almost everyone except me did something similar. I obstinately stayed small. Nobody looked up to me any longer. In that first year the only thing that made me worth knowing was my good marks. The teachers weren't brilliant but they were conscientious. Besides, there was a certain flywheel effect carrying over from Hurstville, where we had been ahead of the curriculum. At the half-yearly examinations I averaged in the high nineties, coming third in the class. Things might have gone on like that for a good while longer if it had not been for Mary Luke.

I was coping with physics and chemistry well enough while Mr Ryan was still teaching them. But Mr Ryan was due for retirement, an event which was hastened by an accident in the laboratory. He was showing us how careful you had to be when handling potassium in the presence of water. Certainly you had to be more careful than he was. The school's entire supply of potassium ignited at once. Wreathed by dense smoke and lit by garish flames, the stunned Mr Ryan looked like a superannuated Greek god in receipt of bad news. The smoke enveloped us all. Windows being thrown open, it jetted into what passed for a playground, where it hung around like some sinister leftover from a battle on the Somme. Shocked, scorched and gassed, Mr Ryan was carried away, never to return.

Back from his third retirement came Mary Luke. A chronic shortage of teachers led to Mary Luke being magically resurrected after each burial. Why he should have been called Mary was a datum lost in antiquity. The school presented him with a pocket watch every time he retired. Perhaps that was a mistake. It might have been the massed ticking that kept him alive. Anyway, Mary Luke, having already ruined science for a whole generation of schoolboys, came back from the shadows to ruin science for me.

Mary was keen but incomprehensible. The first thing he said at the start of every lesson, whether of physics or chemistry, was, 'Make a Bunsen burner.' He was apparently convinced that given the right encouragement we would continue our science studies in makeshift laboratories at home. So we might have done, if we could have understood anything else he said. Unfortunately 'Make a Bunsen burner' was his one remaining fathomable sentence. In all other respects his elocution made my late grandfather sound like Leslie Howard. The same comparison applied to his physical appearance. How could anyone be that old without being dead? But there were definite signs of life. The mouth moved constantly. 'Combustioff off magnesioff,' Mary would announce keenly. 'Magnesioff off oxidoff off hydrogoff off givoff off.' Worriedly I slid the cap off the inverted jar and ignited the gaseous contents to prove that hydrogoff had been givoff off. Carefully I drew the apparatus in my book, already aware that these preliminary experiments would be the last I would ever understand.

Perhaps I was never cut out for chemistry. But I had a right to think that physics might have lain within my scope. I impressed Mary with my precocious knowledge of the planets, which I could name in their order outwards from the sun. Mary looked momentarily blank at the mention of Pluto, but otherwise he seemed well pleased. A novel rearrangement of his lips took place which I guessed to be a smile. The teeth thereby revealed featured eye-catching areas of green amongst the standard amber and ochre. If only we could have stuck to astronomy. Instead, Mary sprang optics on us. 'Thoff angloff off incidoff,' he informed us, 'equoff thoff angloff off reflectioff.' We fiddled dutifully with pins and mirrors. I had the sinking feeling of being unable to understand. The moment of breakdown came when Mary started exploring the different properties of concave and convex mirrors. I couldn't see which was which when he held them up. More importantly,

I couldn't tell the difference when he said their names. 'Thoff miroff off concoff,' he explained carefully, 'off thoff miroff off convoff.' Proud of having made things clear, he smiled fixedly, giving us a long look at his wrecked teeth. What was going *on* in that mouth of his? I could see things moving.

But some of the other boys seemed to understand Mary even if I couldn't, and anyway in the straight mathematical subjects I had no excuse. The teaching might have been uninspired but it was sound enough. Besides, if I had had any mathematical talent I probably wouldn't even have needed teaching. As things were, I remained good at mathematics as long as mathematics remained arithmetic and algebra. I was passable at trigonometry. But when calculus came in, the lights went out. My average marks gradually started to shelve downwards. Things weren't helped by the weekly classes in woodwork and metalwork. I could handle technical drawing well enough, helped by my skill at lettering, but when I entered the workshop I was a gone goose. Metalwork was bad: anything I put in the lathe refused to come out true. It would start off as a cylinder and end up as a blob. So much for my dream of building new jet engines to outclass the Rolls-Royce Avon and the Armstrong Siddeley Sapphire, of designing aircraft whose power and beauty would enrol them among the masterpieces of Sydney Camm, Kurt Tank and Willy Messerschmitt. Woodwork was even worse. Nobody whose hands are not naturally dry can ever be a good carpenter, and I suffered badly from sweaty hands. My hands started to sweat with fear from the moment I put on my calico apron. By the time the woodwork teacher had finished explaining what we had to do my hands would be dripping like taps. Wet hands leave a film on wood that renders it hard to plane. Our first job was to make a breadboard. The breadboard had to be made from half a dozen lengths of wood glued together edge to edge. For this to succeed the edges had to be planed true. I kept on and on from week to week, planing away at my half-dozen pieces. It took me an entire term of classes before I got them true. By that time they were like chopsticks. When I glued my breadboard together it

was the right length but only two inches wide. You couldn't have
cut a French loaf on it.

At the end of second year my average mark was down into the
eighties. Suddenly I had lost my role. Being bright could have saved
me from the ignominy of not growing tall. Growing tall could have
saved me from the ignominy of not being bright. As things were,
I was losing on all counts. In every subject except English and
German I was obviously going nowhere. German was all right for
a while. At Sydney Tech there were only German and French to
choose from. Typically I chose the less beneficial. It was taught by
a huge, shambling teacher we called Lothar, after Mandrake the
Magician's assistant. He was a nice man but charmless. I found it
easy to keep level with Hans Kuckhoff, an immigrant from some
unheard-of country whose family spoke German at home. Kuckhoff
and I shared a desk and compared erections while Lothar concentrated on battering declensions into the heads of the slower boys.
Der den des dem. Die die der der. It was back to the Cubs.

In English I shone – fitfully, but sufficiently to keep my morale
from collapsing altogether. Our teacher in the early years was
'Jazz' Aked. He also doubled as our music teacher: hence the
nickname. 'Jazz' taught English according to the curriculum. The
curriculum was prescriptive. There were grammar, parsing and
Latin roots to be learned. Without resorting to violence, 'Jazz' had
a way of getting results. Eventually I learned to parse any sentence
I was given. I couldn't do it now, but the knowledge is still there
somewhere at an unconscious level. It was invaluable training. On
top of that, he set good essay subjects. My essays were sometimes
read out to the class. I was thereby established all over again as
teacher's pet, but at least it was *something*, in those dreadful days
when everyone else seemed to be doubling in size overnight, while
simultaneously acquiring an Adam's apple like a half-swallowed
rock, a voice like Wallace Beery and a case of acne like the boiling
surface of the sun. Such are the pangs of being left behind – that
you can die of envy for cratered faces weeping with yellow pus.

9. MILO THE MAGNIFICENT

My mother kept on assuring me that I would 'shoot up'. She was not to know I was one of the kind that acquires altitude gradually, with no sudden alteration of the hormonal levels. My testosterone was on a drip feed. In the long run this saved me from anything more revolting than the odd pimple and left me slightly taller than average, but at the time it seemed like a disaster, especially considering that my self-consciousness about girls had abruptly attained new heights, mainly due to the influence of Milo Stefanos. Half the quarry had been sold off as a building block. A house had been built: palatial by our standards, since the garage was under-neath, which effectively gave the place two storeys. The Stefanos family had moved in. Hard-working New Australians, they ran a milk bar down at Brighton, on Botany Bay. Their eldest son, Philip, was already a young man and had attained some renown as a tennis player. Even older than Gary, he was beyond my reach. But their second son, Milo, was my age. He was still in short pants like the rest of us, except that in his case the short pants bulged and pulsed as if he had a live rat stuffed down them. Milo was precocious in every sense.

By now Gary was giving most of his spare time to rebuilding the rusted wreck of a War Department 500cc side-valve BSA that was eventually to become his first motorbike. He had left Kogarah Inter-mediate High School after the Intermediate Certificate and become an apprentice fitter and turner. The balsa-aeroplane days were over. He even left Boys' Brigade. I still visited him a lot and expanded my interest in aeroplanes to an interest in cars and motorbikes. I was buying and memorizing *Flight*, the *Autocar* and the *Motorcycle* every week. At that time they were still substantial publications. I acquired an immense theoretical knowledge. But it was gradually becoming clear to me that theoretical knowledge was not the same as practical capacity. Gary could strip and reassemble a gearbox. All I could do was hand him the spanners. His hands were covered with grease. Cutting oil, I noticed, looked rather like sperm, but opportunities for checking this comparison were growing fewer all the time. Finally it became clear that Gary nowadays preferred doing that sort of thing with girls. Sensitive to my jealousy, he was slow to tell me, but finally the news was too big to hold in. In part recompense for my loss, I was told details. But the girls were Gary's age or older and it all happened somewhere else. There was no hope of joining in.

With Milo it was different. You could get in on all of his adventures, even the supreme one. Milo not only had access to everything, he enjoyed proving it. He had a lot in common with his compatriot Alcibiades. At the back of his garage were stacked hundreds of cartons of cigarettes – stock for the shop. Milo would appropriate the odd carton of Ardath or Craven 'A' to his own use. I thus started smoking at an early age, although it was some years before I dared do it in public. Milo smoked in public while he was still in those challenging short pants. Towards sunset he would appear at the front of the house, his crotch bulging softly in the twilight, and airily smoke a cigarette while combing his hair. Milo combed his hair constantly. Since he smoked constantly too, he spent a lot of time coughing quietly with his eyes screwed up. He looked like a small cloud preening itself. Gathering rapidly like the fast-falling Pacific night, Milo's followers grouped around him. Some of us sat on the front fence. Others did handstands and standing long-jumps on the front strip. Still others rode their bicycles along a complicated route down one of the Margaret Street footpaths and up the other. The route just happened to pass the front of the Chappelows' house, where the girls were gathered. It was rare for the girls actually to join us at that hour. Instead they pretended not to notice, the riders pretending not to notice them.

Meanwhile Milo loaned out examples from his unparalleled collection of Carter Brown detective magazines. Carter Browns were
famous for containing sex scenes. Pale by later standards, this was
nevertheless unmistakably some kind of pornography. Erections
were to be had while reading it.

Most sensationally of all, Milo had access to Laurel Smithers.
Laurel lived in what used to be the house inhabited by the poultry
farmers. Now that the poultry farm was gone and all the land built
over, the old farmhouse on the hill was the only truly ramshackle
house in the district. In effect that meant that it was the only
building for miles which had any aesthetic interest at all, but since
there was nobody within the same radius who had any notion of
what aesthetic interest might happen to be, the house was universally regarded as a blot on the landscape. It had weatherboard walls
and a corrugated-iron roof, upon which, after dark, the missiles of
the Flash of Lightning and his masked companions would often
rain. Quailing under this bombardment, the poultry farmers,
their occupation gone, either died off or moved out, or a mixture
of both. The Smithers family moved in. Mr Smithers spent most of
the day husbanding his energy, while Mrs Smithers pottered about
busying herself with light household tasks, such as breaking stones
with a sledgehammer or forging new springs for the Model 'A'
Ford museum piece they called a car. Laurel was their daughter.
She was Allowed to Run Wild. Yacking over the back fence, our
mothers were agreed, and went on agreeing, that Laurel would
surely Get Into Trouble. They had the right idea, but were using
the wrong tense. Laurel was already seizing every opportunity to
be sexually interfered with by Milo. Indeed interference could
go no further. They were at it continually. The only reason the
adults didn't tumble straight away was that Laurel was already well
embarked on her teens, whereas Milo was only just turning twelve.
They comforted themselves with the thought that Milo would not
know how. They couldn't have been more wrong. Not only did
Milo know how, he was giving lessons.

The word in use was 'root'. Milo used to root Laurel standing up in the back of the garage. He also used to root her lying down in the back of the garage. On special occasions we were all invited to watch. One by one and two by two, half the boys in the district would make their way to Milo's garage on a Saturday afternoon. Inside the garage the atmosphere was tense, mainly because about fifty pairs of lungs were breathing it. Lost in admiration, envy and cigarette smoke, we all watched Milo perform. It was hard to say what Laurel was getting out of it. If she was standing up she looked at us over Milo's heaving shoulders as if we were strangers she was encountering in the street. If she was lying down she looked at the ceiling as if engaged in a long-term entomological study of the spiders inhabiting the rafters. The only evidence that she was not indifferent to the whole process was the way she kept coming back for more.

On very special occasions the rest of us were invited to join in. This only happened when Laurel was 'in the right mood'. If it turned out, after an hour or two of being pounded by Milo, that Laurel was in the right mood, everyone queued up and took a turn. The queue shuffled forward quite rapidly since Laurel would allow even the most fervent admirer only a few seconds inside the sanctum which she had otherwise dedicated to Milo in perpetuity. Only once did I dare join the queue. It was a complete fiasco. The erection which in other circumstances I had so much trouble getting rid of failed to materialize. It was an early instance of First Night Failure, made worse by the fact that it was happening in the early afternoon, when everyone could see – or would have seen, if I had not been so careful to unveil the timorous article only during my last step forward and to rehouse it as soon as I stepped back. Nor was my recalcitrant organ content with merely not inflating. It shrivelled up the way it did after I had been swimming. Laurel was too aphasic to be openly contemptuous. Standing on tiptoe, I pretended to push myself inside her, copying the grunting noises I had heard from Milo and some of the others. It is even possible that Laurel was fooled. I, however, was not.

The incident was just one more piece of evidence bolstering the case for my physical abnormality. When in a state of excitement I could just about convince myself that I was sufficiently well endowed. But to detumesce was the same as to disappear. Other boys seemed to be the same length 'on the slack' as they were when erect, the only difference being that the thing hung down like a length of hose instead of climbing like an extension ladder. Milo, needless to say, was a case in point. On the rare occasions when his uncircumcised tonk was hanging limp, it was still as thick as a third thigh. At full stretch, it was the size of a Japanese midget submarine.

As bad luck would have it, Laurel from then on confined her favours to Milo exclusively, so I never got a second chance. But I still had good reason to be grateful to Milo, since it was in his company that I first came up with something more substantial than a sharp pain and a puff of air. As a masturbator Milo was if anything even more impressive than as a lover. Smoking casually with one hand, he employed the other to stimulate himself, his only problem being how to choose the most satisfactory grip. If he held the near end there was apparently a certain loss of sensitivity, so that the process might occupy a minute or even more. If he held the far end he could get results in a matter of seconds, but his arm would be at full stretch. There was no mistaking the moment when Milo was on the point of unburdening himself. You could practically hear the stuff coming. He could have put out a fire with it. With due allowance for scale, I was matching him stroke for stroke one day when suddenly I produced something. It was the only clear-cut sign of puberty I was ever to be vouchsafed. My pride knew no bounds. Even Milo was impressed – a generous reaction, since the stuff was all over one of his best Carter Browns. But the change of status might as well have been metaphysical for all the difference it made to the size of my dick when dormant. At school this problem aggravated all my other problems. After our PT sessions I lingered elaborately in the changing room so that I could duck into the communal shower after everybody else had come out. If I could manage a semi-erection everything was all right. I didn't mind joining in the towel-flicking if I had something to show. Unfortunately a semi-erection is no more easily achieved by will than a full-sized version. So I had to do a great deal of loitering.

It was an eternal anxiety. In a class full of cock-watchers, I had to keep something between my shrinking twig and a hundred prying eyes, all the while contriving the deception so that it never seemed deliberate. Emerging from the shower with a towel draped casually around me, I had to put on my underpants before I took off the towel, but make it look as if I was taking off the towel before I put on my underpants. The result was a Gypsy Rose Lee routine of extraordinary subtlety. I calculated the sight lines and the lighting like Max Reinhardt or the Black Theatre of Prague. Either I was never spotted, or what I had down there looked less underprivileged than I thought. According to Hemingway, when Scott Fitzgerald proclaimed himself worried about the size of his tool (and we have only Hemingway's hopelessly unreliable word that this ever happened) the tall writer told the short writer that anybody's prong looks small when the owner looks down on it. On behalf of my younger self I would like to agree, but at the time I spent many an anxious hour in front of my bedroom mirror and there could be no doubt that my tossle looked the same from the side as it did from on top – i.e., like a shy silkworm.

As self-consciousness approached its dizzy peak, I spent so much of my spare time checking up on myself in mirrors that there was hardly any left over for little matters like homework. A dressing table, strangely enough, was among the few pieces of furniture in my room, which by now was a small library of books about aircraft, cars, motorcycles and war. The table beside my bed, which had previously housed my laboratory – which is to say, the collection of malodorous junk I had brought back from the dump – was now stacked with carefully filed and cross-referenced technical magazines. The cupboard off which we had all once dived onto the bed was now mainly a bookcase, in which such titles as *The Dam Busters* and *Reach for the Sky* took pride of place. On the walls, which my mother had tolerantly always allowed me to decorate as

I pleased, coloured tracings of Disney characters had been joined by elaborate cut-away drawings of aircraft, so that you had a Dornier Do. 17 unloading its bombs on Donald Duck. The room was like the cell of a machine-mad monk. The only human touch was the half-length portrait on one wall, which turned out on closer examination to be the dressing-table mirror containing my reflection. Almost always the reflection was in profile, as I held up a hand mirror at an angle in front of me in order to see what I looked like from the side. Why did the back of my head stick out so far? Why did my jaw stick out so little? As all the boys around me started turning into men, I began to wonder if perhaps I was not doomed to look boyish for ever.

Even at its best, Sydney Tech was simply a waste of time. But even at its worst, it mainly just got me down, rather than driving me to despair. Had it been a boarding school I would probably have been in real trouble. As things were, most of my agonies were self-inflicted through an excess of inward-turned imagination. Unfortunately misery is not relative. For some reason the school prided itself on its achievements in rugby union. It always finished high in the CHS competitions and occasionally fielded a team which could lick the best of the GPS teams, although Sydney High always remained the unbeatable enemy. For most of my school career I was obliged to play House football, which was a joke. The very idea of dividing the school into houses was another joke. I was a member of Williams House. Nobody seemed to be bothered by the fact that no building existed which could be described as Williams House or even Williams Hut. In fact Williams House consisted exclusively of the yellow singlets its members wore during athletics competitions. Dyed at home by mothers commanding various techniques and materials, the singlets covered the range of all possible yellows from fresh butter to old urine. Wearing mine, I came third in the heats and second last in the finals. Once I had been a fast runner, but that was before I started to shrink.

House football took place in a park only a few miles' brisk march from the school. As a cold wind whipped across the grass, the two teams would position themselves in expectation of the opening whistle. The start of each half was the only time when the eye could detect even an approximation of positional sense. The moment the whistle blew, thirty small boys would gather around the ball, forming a compact, writhing, many-legged mound which during the course of what seemed like hours would transfer itself at random to different parts of the field. I was somewhere in the middle, praying it would end.

But there was worse to come. On days when a Grade football team had a bye, its members would be brought to our park so that they could practise dodging tackles. They ran down the field while we tried to tackle them. It went without saying that they were bigger, faster and more skilful than we were. The real nightmare was when the First Grade side turned up. The star of First Grade was Reg Gasnier, already tipped as the brightest schoolboy rugby prospect in years. Indeed he toured England the following year with the Australian Rugby League side. Merely to watch Gasnier run was to die a little. He was all knees and elbows. His feet scythed outwards as he ran, like Boadicea's hubcaps. There seemed no way of tackling him without sustaining a compound fracture. Up and down the field he steamed while we ran at him from different angles, only to bounce off, fall stunned, or miss completely as he sidestepped. He was beautiful to watch if you weren't among the prospective victims. The way he shifted his weight in one direction while swerving in the other was a kind of poetry. Regrettably it was also very painful if experienced at close quarters. I can well remember the first time I was deputed to tackle Gasnier. He was three times as heavy as I was, although, density having the relationship it does to dimensions, he was of course only twice as high. There were only a couple of hundred people watching. Gasnier appeared out of the distance like an express train moving unhampered by rails. I ran at him on a despairing collision course. Casually he put his hand in my face. My head stopped while the rest of me kept going, so that I spent a certain amount of time supine in midair before falling deftly on my back. While I was being resuscitated on the sidelines, Gasnier kindly materialized in my blurred vision and explained that the thing to do was keep my head low so that he could not palm me off. The next time I tackled him I kept my head low. Sidestepping with uncanny ease, he put his hand on the back of my head and pushed my face into the ground. So much for the friendly advice. When they picked me up, or rather pulled me out, there was an impression of my face in the turf that you could have made a plaster cast from. It would have looked disappointed but resigned.

None of this would have mattered if I could have kept up with the swimmers. Swimming had, after all, always been my best thing. The hours and days spent in the creek and the Dom with the Meldrums had paid off in a certain fluency of style. When I was twelve years old I used to hold my own in races across the creek against a local boy who subsequently was to take the silver medal for the hundred metres freestyle at the Melbourne Olympics. At the time when I could keep up with him we were the same size. By the time of the Olympics he was six feet three inches tall and could close his hand around the grips of two tennis rackets. But it wasn't just a matter of height. There was the question of attitude. I simply found excuses never to start training. After Mr Meldrum's death, and with Gary playing a less important part in my life, I felt able to attend Ramsgate Baths on the weekends. Ramsgate Baths was a set of tiled pools fed by seawater from Botany Bay. Since the water was confined and remained unchanged for days on end, Mr Meldrum had frowned on Ramsgate Baths as unhealthy. He was, of course, absolutely right. The water in each pool would be green on the first day, orange on the second day and saffron the third. The whole place was one vast urinal. But there were diving boards, sand pits and giggling swarms of girls wearing Speedo swimming costumes. The Speedo was a thin, dark-blue cotton one-piece affair whose shoulder straps some of the girls tied together behind with a ribbon so as to tauten the fabric over their pretty bosoms. On a correctly formed pubescent girl a Speedo looked wonderful, even when it was dry. When it was wet, it was an incitement to riot.

At Ramsgate Baths, weekend after weekend, year after year, I would show off with the clown diving troupe, dive-bomb near the edge of the pool to drench the girls, do mildly difficult acrobatic tricks, smoke and comb my hair. There were a whole bunch of us who wasted all our time in this fashion. We were masters of the flat racing dive and the quick, flashy fifty-five yards. Any one of us would have sunk like a rock had he attempted a second lap, but we could all do an impressive tumble turn. When the whistle blew for races and the real swimmers appeared in their tracksuits, we repaired to the sandpit, there to tell what we imagined were dirty jokes and share a fanatically casual cigarette with the more daring girls. Erections were either hidden or flaunted, depending on one's reputation for effrontery. I hid mine, either by draping a towel over my trunks as additional camouflage or just lying prone in the sand until the embarrassing acquisition went away. Sometimes this took a whole afternoon, but there was certainly nothing better to do. Falling for – not just perving on, but actually and rackingly falling for – a pretty girl in a Speedo certainly beat any thrills that were being experienced by the poor bastards who were swimming themselves to jelly in the heats and semi-finals. So, at any rate, I supposed. Every few minutes you could hear the spectators roar as they goaded some half-wit onward to evanescent glory. Meanwhile I concentrated on the eternal values of the way a girl's nipples hardened against her will behind their veils of blue cotton, or the way the sweet skin of her thigh near the groin might be the vellum mounting for a single black hair like the escaped mainspring of a pygmy timepiece.

The same sort of dichotomy prevailed at school. The school swimming team trained hard at North Sydney Olympic Pool. The rest of us went by toast-rack tram to Rushcutter's Bay, Redleaf Pool, Bronte or Coogee. The first two were small net enclosures in Sydney Harbour: they offered little except weeds around your legs and the constant challenge of dodging jelly-blubbers. But Bronte and Coogee pools were both beside ocean beaches, so that after the regulation hour of splashing around to no purpose and/or practising for the Bronze Medallion you could change back into uniform, have your name ticked off the roll, rush down to the dressing rooms on the beach, change back into trunks and head for the surf. The first pair of flippers made their appearance in those years. I had a big pair of green adjustables with straps that hurt – a characteristically bad buy – but I could catch waves with them well enough. Afraid of sharks but pleased to be at one with the elements, I surfed until I was exhausted. There were half a dozen of us, wastrels all, who thus used to consume the spare hours of every Wednesday afternoon after compulsory swimming – the beauty of our activities being, needless to say, that they were not compulsory. Frank Griffiths was our master spirit. Like Milo he was something of a lurk-man, but he had the additional quality of humour. In class he used to charm his way out of trouble. I began to see that there were advantages to playing the fool. In the surf he was completely at home. His skin was as slick as a duck's feathers. Broad-shouldered and long-legged, he could have been a competition swimmer if he had wanted to. But he didn't want to, any more than the rest of us.

For one thing, it was too much like work. For another, even if you did the work there was no guarantee of success. The best swimmer in our school was Peter Case. He trained about a hundred miles a day. He had gills. Every year from first year through to fifth he was champion. But he never finished higher than fourth in the CHS carnival. One year I watched him at North Sydney Olympic pool. He was in the same 440 race as Jon Henricks, who was then at Fort Street, and already well on the way to his Olympic gold. Henricks won by almost a length of the pool. Case was impressive to watch but you could see the strain. Henricks seemed to expend no effort whatsoever. He glided frictionless, as if salt water were interstellar space. Each arm was perfectly relaxed as it reached forward over the water, stiffening only when it became immersed. Each of his lazily waving feet seemed a third long section of the leg to which it was so loosely attached. The bow wave in front of his nose curved downwards on its way back, leaving a trough of air in which he occasionally breathed. He annihilated distance at a rate of about twenty strokes to the lap and tumble-turned like a porpoise running between wickets. He swam as if dreaming. It was clear that he had been born to swim. There was no point in even trying to compete. Contrary to the pious belief, where sports are concerned the important thing is not to have taken part, but to have won.

Nevertheless Case and his fellow swimmers, together with all the other star athletes, formed an elite within the school no matter how mediocre their performances outside it. If Case was worshipped, you can imagine what happened when John Konrads arrived. Even in his first year he was already nearly six feet tall. Still only eleven years old, he broke the school senior 880 record at his first carnival. He would have won every other senior event if he had been allowed to compete, but the 880 was the only one he was allowed to enter, and then only because there was no race at that distance in his age group. Upon being lapped for the second time, Case – then in his fifth and final year – retired with a broken heart and headed for the showers, the only healthy man I have ever seen limping with both legs. Not long afterwards Konrads went on to capture a sheaf of world records and become recognized as the greatest male swimmer on Earth. I am pleased to report, however, jumping ahead a bit, that in my last year at Sydney Tech I was privileged, in my capacity as prefect, to book him for running in the playground.

10. THE SOUND OF MUCUS

Even if I had possessed the will and the weight to be an athlete, an essential part of the wherewithal would still have been missing. Although I looked in the bloom of health, I was racked by colds throughout my adolescence. Indeed it was just one long cold that never went away. I produced mucus in thick streams. I carried half a dozen handkerchiefs and they were all full by the end of the day. Kleenex had already been invented but had not yet penetrated to Kogarah, where people still put a cold in their pockets. I was putting an epidemic in mine. Finally the floods of green slime and the interminable sniffle drove my mother to consult the local GP, Dr Bolton, who prescribed a course of penicillin injections. Over the next few years I was shot full of millions of units of penicillin. I built up a tremendous resistance to penicillin and an unquenchable fear of the hypodermic syringe – the latter phobia being destined to become a key factor, later on, in my long truancy from the dentist. I shook at the mere idea of being stuck. The actuality should have been just a dull thud in the upper arm, but I tensed up so much that the needle bounced off. Dr Bolton had to screw it in like a bradawl.

This went on for a couple of years with no diminution in the snot supply. Quite the contrary. No matter how hard I blew there was always more up there. This unabated deliquescence was gradually joined by such additional features as sharp pains above and behind the eyes. At the baths I couldn't submerge more than a few feet without feeling the extra pressure. Rather fancying myself as a diver, I was disappointed to find myself confined to the one-metre board. Not that I would ever have accomplished much from the

three-metre board – an innate lack of daring guaranteed that – but
one of my chief pleasures in life was to descend from a great height
and somersault while making contact with the water at the very lip
of the pool. This activity was known as dive-bombing. An expert
could make an impact like a 500-pounder, saturating the spectators
over a range of many yards. There came a day when I surfaced in
the puddle of spume produced by a particularly effective dive-
bomb, and found my face hurting so much I could hardly get out
of the water. For a while I thought that I had hit the tiled edge of
the pool with my head.

Dr Bolton finally decided that my sinuses needed a wash. First
he probed them extensively, using a stick wrapped in cotton wool
soaked with local anaesthetic. This was the least funny thing that
had ever happened to me, not excluding the time when I had had
an abscessed tooth extracted and been sneered at by the dentist
merely because a spout of pus had hit him in the eye. Dr Bolton's
immortal line, 'You may feel a bit of discomfort,' still strikes me
today as ranking among the understatements of the century. In a
way he was right. What I felt wasn't pain so much as pressure. It
was as if a wardrobe were being crammed up my nose. When he
yanked out the stick and started to sluice the violated interior,
I began a sobbing fit that lasted for some time. I went home
traumatized. After visits to the dentist I usually tucked into a packet
of Minties and a few bars of Cherry Ripe, secure in the knowledge
that it would be a year before I had to go again. But with the
sinuses I was on constant call. I had to keep up the treatment.
Dr Bolton went on probing and sluicing for what seemed to me
like years, until one day, on his way up my nose, he met a polyp
coming down.

Polyps, or proud flesh, apparently favour the sinuses as growth
areas. If I stuck my finger up my left nostril I could feel it entirely
blocked by a convex meniscus the texture of Bakelite. This was the
vanwall of what Dr Bolton assured my mother could be anything
between a platoon and a battalion of polyps. Dr Bolton also assured
her that a simple operation under local anaesthetic would be

enough to clear the matter up. My mother, strongly supported by a silent tantrum I was staging in the background, suggested that I might be spared some suffering if the operation was done under general anaesthetic. 'No need for that,' Dr Bolton assured her. 'He'll only feel a bit of discomfort.'

After only a few weeks of sleepless waiting I found myself seated in Dr Bolton's surgery. Dressed in a white coat, he was on another chair facing me. First he did the familiar number with the dope-soaked stick of fairy floss. I found this as hilarious as always. Then he got up there with a pair of long-nosed forceps. They were slim to look at but by the time they were in my head they felt like heavy wire-cutters. It all lasted for centuries and I did a lot of crying. When I glanced into the kidney-shaped enamel basin on the table, it was heaped high with what would have looked like freshly cooked tripe if it had not been streaked with blood. My mother was waiting in the reception room when I came out. She had an awful look on her face. I have learned to recognize that look since. It is the way we look when someone we love is suffering and we can't help.

The operation was so traumatic that I spent the next year doing my best to conceal the fact that it had not worked. But there was too much mucus to hide and the pain both above and below my eyes formed a pair of invisible hot iron spectacles that kept me awake. Dr Bolton at last referred me to a specialist. He, too, was fond of a preliminary probe or two with the fairy floss, but at least this time there was not a suggestion that the operation should be a sit-down. He wanted me down and out. I have never minded general anaesthetic. I rather relish the dreams. When I woke up, my head felt clear for the first time in years – perhaps the first time ever, since I could not remember when I had ever breathed so easily. There was some heavy bleeding, which the specialist staunched by stuffing my facial cavities full of gauze. This was only mildly amusing and the removal of the blood-caked gauze a few days later was even less so, but my new-found happiness was unimpaired. I went on suffering more than my share of colds, but the bad days ended with that operation. I can still remember the specialist's kindly look. Dr Bolton, who assisted at the operation, told me later that he had never seen such instruments: some of them had had little lights on them.

That has been the sum total of my ill-health to date: one adolescent brush with sinusitis. I didn't even have a severe case. To cure Joan Sutherland of the same thing, they had to slice her open along the top gum and cut through the bone behind her face. So I got off lightly. But the feeling of being helplessly dependent on medical skills is one I have never forgotten. Only in thoughtless moments do I take my strong constitution for granted. When I see sick, crippled or deformed people in the street, I always feel that the reason why they have too little luck is that someone gave me too much.

My hopes of heroism fading, I was obliged to find a new role, especially when I started ceasing to be a star even at English. 'Jazz' moved on, a martinet came in and I froze up. I was still near the top of the class, owing to my unusual powers of parsing, but I hardly stood out. Luckily a certain gift of the gab opened the way to a new career as a joker. The small boy is usually obliged to be amusing just as the fat boy is usually obliged to be amiable. I cultivated a knack of exaggeration. Lying outrageously, I inflated rumour and hearsay into saga and legend. The price of fame was small but decisive. I had to incur the accusation of being a bull artist – a charge that any Australian male of any age wants to avoid. But I wanted notoriety more. Rapidly I acquired it. From a small circle of listeners in class, I progressed to a large circle of listeners in the playground. Bigger boys came to mock and stayed to listen. Adapted from a recently seen film, my story of the Okinawa kamikazes lasted an entire lunchtime and drew an audience which, if it had not come equipped with its own sandwiches, would have had to be fed with loaves and fishes.

My new line in yarn-spinning was an expansion of the same trick that I had been working in Sunday School. All I had done was throw caution to the winds. I had also mastered the art of laughing at myself a fraction of a second before anybody else did. Climaxing a story of my close personal acquaintance with Rommel, I produced a pair of old sand-goggles from my pocket. This convinced the smaller boys, but the older boys were not fooled. Before they could laugh, I beat them to it. I ran with the hares, hunted with the hounds and never left a swing except to step onto a roundabout. Gradually even the most scornful among my listeners came to accept that what Jamesie said wasn't *meant* to be true – only entertaining. If it wasn't that, key figures drifted away, and soon everyone else was gone along with them, leaving me alone with my uneaten sandwiches. It was my first experience of the difference between clicking and flopping.

Riding the crest, I diversified, exploiting a highly marketable capacity to fart at will. Thus I became an all-round entertainer. Somehow, perhaps by osmosis, I had learned this invaluable knack from Milo, who could fart the opening bars of 'Blue Moon'. The first time he performed this feat to a select audience in the back of his garage, the effect was shattering. Suddenly we were all outside in the sunlight, staggering around gasping with combined suffocation and astonishment. Using the Zippo cigarette lighter he had stolen from his father, Milo would set a light to his farts, producing a jet of flame rivalling that emitted by the oil refinery at Kurnell, across the bay. I was never able to match Milo for sonority and melodic content, but I did manage to acquire the knack of letting one off whenever I wanted to. By mastering this skill I set myself on a par with those court jesters of old who could wow the monarch and all his retinue by unleashing, as a grandstand finale, a simultaneous leap, whistle and fart. Unable to extend my neo-Homeric storytelling activities from the playground to the classroom, I could nevertheless continue to hog the limelight by interpolating a gaseous running commentary while the teacher addressed himself to the blackboard. The essential factor here was volume control. My contributions had to be loud enough to amuse the class but not so strident that they caught the teacher's ear. They were bound to catch his nose eventually, but by that time they were untraceable, since I never made the mistake of either looking proud or overdoing the angelic innocence. While the teacher stood there with his nostrils twitching and scanned the room for malefactors, I stared inscrutably into the middle distance, as if lost in the middle of a quadratic equation.

Two bacon rolls and a custard pie were my undoing. Tuck-shop lunches were a dangerous substitute for home-cut sandwiches, since they generated a less controllable supply of wind. Fred Pickett, the best of our maths teachers, was filling the board with some incomprehensible account of what happened to a locus on its way up the abscissa. I was waiting for a suitable cue. The whole secret of raising a laugh with a fart in class is to make it sound as if it is punctuating, or commenting upon, what the teacher is saying. Timing, not ripeness, is all. 'And since x tends to y as c tends to d,' Fred expounded, 'then the differential of the increment of x squared must be ... must be ... come on, come *on*! What must it flaming *be*!' Here was a chance to give my version of what it must be. I armed one, opened the bomb bay and let it go. Unfortunately the results far exceeded the discreet limits I had intended. It sounded like a moose coughing. The shockwave and gamma radiation left people in nearby desks leaning sideways with both hands over their noses. Picking up a blackboard duster, Fred spun round, took aim and hurled it with one flowing movement. There was no question about his choice of target. Concentric circles of outward-leaning victims pointed back to me as surely as all those felled trees in Siberia pointed back to the meteor's point of impact. The duster impinged tangentially on my cranium and clattered to the floor. Within seconds I was on my way to the deputy headmaster. I was carrying a note inscribed with the numeral 6, meaning that I was to be given six of the best.

The deputy head, Mr Dock, inevitably known as Hickory, lacked inches but made up for them with agility. A short, round man, he had a long, thin, whippy cane and would have looked like Bobby Riggs serving an ace if he had not prefaced his wind-up and delivery with a short swerving run starting in the far corner of the room. He didn't waste time talking. He just opened the note, glanced at it and reached for the cane. Suddenly I wanted desperately to urinate. 'C-c-c-c-c-can I go to the t-t-t-t-toi-toi-toilet?' I asked bravely. To his great credit Hickory let me go. Perhaps he was not the psychopath he was cracked up to be. Perhaps he just didn't want a puddle on his floor. I raced downstairs and made it to the urinal approximately in time. My return up the same stairs was glacial, nay asymptotic, but Hickory kindly appeared on the landing to encourage me over the final stages. Since the rules stipulated that the hands be hit alternately, for each stroke Hickory had to change corners of the room before running up to serve. He covered a lot of ground. I found the shock of each impact nothing like as bad as the anticipation. Unfortunately the aftermath was worse than anything that could be imagined. I zigzagged back to class with my hands buried between my thighs. But even in the midst of my agony, I was already secure in the knowledge that fame was assured.

11. A PRONG IN PERIL

Thus I served out my remaining years at school – as a clown. It never made me especially popular, but at least I avoided unpopularity. At the end of each school year it was a bespectacled owl called Schratah who got tied to the flagpole and pelted with cream cakes. The most I can say for myself is that I didn't throw any of the cakes. But I can't pretend that I wasn't glad somebody else was being picked on instead of me. I would have found victimization hard to bear. Why Schratah didn't commit suicide was a constant mystery to me. It wasn't, after all, that they hated him for being Jewish and a foreigner. They hated him for himself.

Never shooting up with the suddenness I had been promised, I never stopped gradually growing either, until eventually it dawned on me that I was as tall as everyone else, with the necessary exception of the athletic heroes. Still checking up in the mirror, I came to realize that my neck was now if anything thicker than my head, although the back of my skull still protruded instead of sloping forward like Superman's. There had also been a mildly encouraging improvement in the behaviour of my tool. After prolonged immersion it still shrivelled up to the size of a jellybean, but otherwise – although I was in no danger of standing on the end of it – it was at least visible. Indeed nowadays it seemed always to be in one of two conditions: erect and semi-erect. The Smithers family had moved hurriedly away, amid rumours that Milo had finally and irrevocably Got Laurel Into Trouble. It didn't occur to me, or probably even to Milo, that such things could be attempted with any other girl except her. Ordinary girls could be kissed and fiddled with but there was no question of Going All The

Way. Australia was still one of the most strictly moralistic societies in the Western world. As a natural corollary, rape was endemic. Every day and ten times on Sundays, the tabloid newspapers carried stories of young men being sentenced to life imprisonment for rape. Most of them seemed to deserve it, but sometimes you wondered. I was especially impressed by the front-page stories about a young photographer who had taken twelve models down into the National Park near Heathcote and raped them all. Apparently he rendered them helpless with a roll of Elastoplast, releasing them one at a time from bondage in order to slake his fell desires. It occurred to me that either the young man or the Elastoplast must have had magic properties. But if the same thing ever occurred to the judge and jury, there was no hint of it. The rapist was taken to Goulbourn jail and locked up to begin paying the slow price of his depravity. He's probably still there now.

Margaret, in the next street, would let me kiss her. Her mouth seemed to be always full of water and she had a way of bumping your teeth with hers, so that you were spitting chips of enamel afterwards, but she felt round and warm to hold, if you didn't mind the dribble. Jan, across the street, was pointedly eager to be kissed and even mildly interfered with, but her eyes crossed so badly that you kept wondering if she had seen something in the distance – a police car, for example. Shirley, down the street, was the most exciting of the local girls. At spin-the-bottle parties she was the number-one target. She had a fully developed figure and a marvellous hot, yielding mouth. I spent half an hour kissing her one night, pinning her against the wall in the driveway of her house. I had to go home in a running crouch, like a black-tracker. Shirley was so passionate that she might have cooperated if one of us had seriously tried to seduce her. But nobody our age had the nerve. It was an older boy from another district who had the privilege of taking Shirley's virginity, which must have felt as clean and crisp as the first bite of a sweet apple. His name was Barry Tate. Sensationally in command of his own car – a black Hillman Minx – he came booming down the street each evening after another easy day's work doing whatever it was he did. He had a concave chest and a rich, multi-coloured collection of pimples, but there was no getting past the fact that he also had his own car. He would take Shirley away in it to park down among the dunes at Doll's Point or Ramsgate. Somewhere out there, a long way beyond our envious reach, she must have yielded him her all. Apart from Boys' Brigade, in which I became a less and less prominent participant, my church activities took up a steadily greater proportion of my spare time, principally because there were girls involved. I had one case of the amorous vision after another. Once I had graduated into long trousers, I even felt it possible to translate such adoration into real acquaintanceship. Christine Ballantine, alas, was beyond my hopes. She was almost beyond even my dreams. Short in the leg but unbelievably lovely in the face, she looked like the top half of a Botticelli angel. I burned tunnels in the air adoring her from afar. I even slogged through church twice in an evening, just to look at her as she sat in the choir. This was no mean tribute to her beauty, since the second sitting of church included a full-scale sermon from the Rev. C. Cummings Campbell. Quoting liberally from *A Man Called Peter* and various religious savants with three names each, the Rev. Campbell would unload from the pulpit a seemingly fathomless cargo of clichés. Meanwhile I drank in Christine's beauty, its every movement of lip and eyelid more pleasing to God than anything the Rev. Campbell would ever say.

Little Sandra McDougall I actually managed to touch. She was a tiny, sweet-looking blonde with a deep, grating voice like Mr Chifley, the late lamented leader of the Labor Party. The standard heavy teasing informed her of my love. With shyness on my side and understandable reluctance on hers, we got to the hand-holding stage. Unfortunately my sinuses, not yet cured at that time, ruined everything. No sooner had I picked up her white-gloved hand than I had to put it down again in order to blow my nose in whatever section of my sodden handkerchief had been used least. Behind the veil depending from her frangipani-bedecked hat, her large blue eyes would shut in what I hoped was modest sympathy, but suspected to be disgust. Eventually she took to tapping her foot while I honked and hooted. Finally she turned away.

But later on, with my health improved, the end of school approaching and some recognizable version of late adolescence approaching along with it, I began to find some of the older girls not entirely averse to being fumbled with. This was a revelation. That a mad girl like Laurel might do everything made it seem more likely, not less, that ordinary well-brought-up girls would do nothing. And yet here they were, letting you put your hand on their breasts or even – in advanced cases – between their thighs. It was a kind of warfare, with no-go areas and free-fire zones. Breast fondling could go on for some time, but when it noticeably led to a deeper stage of heavy breathing then it had to stop. Thigh stroking could go on for only a short time at one go, although the hand was allowed back again at a decent interval after removal. A really determined assault might have burst through all these conventions but I would probably have been scared to death if they had suddenly ceased to be operative. Carol Pascoe, for example, didn't seem to know the rules. There was always a race to take her home after Fellowship meetings or socials. A few times I won it, usually by booking her up a week in advance. She had no inclination to remove the exploratory hand or even, as I was stunned to discover, the exploratory finger, which could work its will unchecked until numbness set in, leaving you with the disturbing sensation of having only nine fingers left. Meanwhile Carol would be bumping and grinding with her mouth open and her eyes closed. It was vaguely frightening, although one of course pretended otherwise. A dozen of us, comparing notes, loudly agreed that Carol was the Best to Take Home. Reg Hook showed us the condom that he planned to use on her. He had a detailed plan to dispel what was left of her innocence. As Reg later recounted it, the plan – involving himself, Carol, a blanket and a Doll's Point sand dune at midnight – unfolded with ridiculous ease. In a trice Carol was lying there, sobbing with need. Unfortunately Reg was under the impression that you had to unroll the condom before putting it on. Since the rest of us would have done the same in his place, we were hardly in a position to point out his mistake.

Eventually a Scottish immigrant boy called Dorber gave Carol what she wanted. Thick of accent, repellent of epidermis and wise in the ways of the Glasgow slums, Dorber was an unlikely member of Fellowship or indeed of any organization more benign than the Parachute Regiment. But then he was not in search of religious instruction. He was out to use what we had been wasting. Our idea of the successful climax to an exciting evening was to limp home with a throbbing crotch and a finger smelling like a fishing smack. Dorber's ambitions were less oblique. He wanted everything, and in several cases, to our flabbergasted disapproval, got it. Still, at least I had some tangible evidence that I was normally endowed. The only problem was to find the opportunity, courage and purpose which would allow of the endowment being put to use. The problem was almost solved for ever during a fortnight away at a National Fitness camp somewhere up in the bush. I attended this camp as part of a Sydney Tech contingent which included Griffiths and others among the freaks and wastrels. I never bothered to find out at the time precisely what National Fitness was or what aims it was supposed to pursue, but in retrospect I can see that it was a reasonably benevolent outfit promoting the concept of *mens sana in corpore sano* on what it imagined to be an international scale. The camp, constructed along military lines, consisted of weatherboard huts scattered through the bush and linked up with winding paths. There were several hundred boys present, including a hefty representation from Nauru Island. So black they looked blue, these were some of the best-looking boys in creation. The one to whom all the others deferred, although never with servility, was Detudame, son of the Chief of Nauru.

Nowadays, Detudame is chief himself. I saw him on television recently and was pleased to note that he had acquired a weight problem closely resembling my own. At the time I am talking about he was already pretty bulky, but it was all dark muscle, subtly catching tangential light like polished hardwood. His retinue called him Det for short. Within minutes we all did. He had Napoleonic charisma combined with infinite charm. Through the black and white crowd that surrounded him at all times I snatched glimpses from a distance, awed by the amusement that spontaneously came into being around him and which he could silence with a frown. He and the Nauruans played a strip-tease game in which the object was to keep your clothes while all around you were losing theirs. While he was doing the same to you, you whipped your hands suddenly from behind your back and confronted your opponent with any one of three symbols: scissors, paper, rock. Scissors cut paper but broke on rock. Paper covered rock but was cut by scissors. If you lost, you had to remove an article of clothing, even if it was the last thing you had on. When Det lost – which he seldom did, being a mind-reader – he stripped just as willingly as his subjects. But on the one occasion when he was forced down as far as his underpants, he insisted on going behind a bush. While his entourage rolled around in hysterics, all we saw was the royal Y-fronts being waved in the air. Thus the future monarch's dignity was preserved. It will be apparent that I am talking about the kind of brother I would have liked to have, and I suppose miss even now.

This is a generous appreciation on my part, considering that Det and his friends brought me to the edge of catastrophe. One night we were playing Hunt the Lantern. I forget the rules. Probably I have repressed them. The relevant facts are simple. I was fleeing at full tilt through the pitch dark on a zigzag path between the gum trees. Det and a couple of his more carnivorous-looking pals were after me. Equipped with excellent night vision and the ability to run silently even over dead leaves, they were bad dreams straight out of James Fenimore Cooper. Suddenly I heard Det's voice shouting at me to look out. I thought it was a ruse and crammed on more speed. With stunning abruptness some kind of silent landmine blew me straight up in the air. The stars raced past my eyes in parallel streaks, like the tips of porcupine quills. I landed sitting down, having performed the best part of a double forward somersault in the piked, or wrecked, position. Det and his friends arrived, vaulting unerringly over the barbed-wire fence that I had just tried to run through.

The fence had had three strands. The top strand had caused a certain amount of damage across my lower chest. The bottom strand had torn a few holes in my upper shins and knees. The middle strand had apparently done nothing more than tear my khaki shorts across the crotch. When they got me to the first-aid centre it was soon agreed that the shock was a worse threat than the cuts. The cuts were treated with the mandatory daubing of Acriflavine, tufts of cotton wool being left on the wounds so that scabs would form neatly under the gauze bandages. The shock was treated by wrapping me in a blanket and leaving me there to spend the night. When everyone was gone I reached up, switched the light back on and snuck a look under my shorts. I had discouraged all attempts to remove them, but it couldn't be denied that a dull ache was emanating from that area. What I had felt, however, paled beside what I now saw. My tonk was sliced open on one side to what looked like a mortal depth. It was as if the captain of the *Titanic*, a few minutes after the encounter with the iceberg, had been lowered by the heels and given a sudden underwater close-up of the trouble he was in. The wound wasn't bleeding. It was just gaping. Hurriedly I covered it up again and stared at the ceiling, simultaneously pretending I hadn't seen what I had seen and wondering desperately what to do.

I chose to do nothing. In the event this proved to be the right decision, but it was prompted by nothing except cowardice. The mere thought of a doctor putting stitches in my tossle made me cross and uncross my legs very rapidly – or would have done, had I dared move them. So for days on end I kept my secret, snatching a look at the disaster area as often as I could. It was inspiring to see how quickly the antibodies rallied to the task. It was like a speeded-up film. Rapidly the whole area turned bright white, then pink. The gash itself, after first filling up with dark blood, tightened into a crisp scab that clicked satisfactorily when I tapped it with a fingernail. Before the remaining week of camp was over, it was obvious that my much-abused saveloy was out of danger. Even at this time, this was a relief. Looking back, I almost faint at the sheer range of implication. Another quarter of an inch on those barbs and my subsequent love life would have consisted entirely of bad scenes from *The Sun Also Rises*.

12. ALL DRESSED UP

As the final years of school flowed turgidly under the bridge I became increasingly lost. Now that I had at last grown up, my comic persona no longer quite fitted. For many years I was to remain a prisoner of my own, like a ventriloquist taken over by his dummy. Even today, unless I watch myself carefully, I take refuge in levity. Only self-discipline keeps my face straight. In *War and Peace*, if I were not allowed to identify with Andrey or even Nikolai then I suppose I would settle for Dolokhov. I would even try to be pleased if it were pointed out that I was in fact Pierre. But the man I can't help recognizing myself in is the unfortunate Zherkovim, who makes an untimely joke about the defeated General Mack and receives the full blast of Andrey's wrath.

Anyway, there is no point in carping now. My clever lip won me whatever popularity was coming to me at the time, so that I was able to go on finding myself welcome, or not unwelcome, among Griffiths' surfing parties and the school YMCA team that competed annually for the Pepsi-Cola Shield. Indeed among the latter crew I at last found myself a measure of sporting stardom, since the vaulting I had so painfully learned at Boys' Brigade was something of an advance on anything the other Centurions (that was the name of our team) could improvise uninstructed. My feet-through and flying angel-roll on the long box were instrumental in bringing the Pepsi-Cola Shield home to Sydney Technical High – a fact duly announced at school assembly. It didn't sound much of an achievement (and in fact was even less of an achievement than it sounded, since the teams we had defeated looked like pages from a Unesco pamphlet about the ravages of vitamin deficiency) but it was something. I also managed, at the eleventh hour, to be chosen for Grade football. It was only Third Grade, which consisted mainly of rejects from Second Grade, but you were given a fifth-hand jersey to wear and travelled about, meeting similarly decrepit sides from other schools. My position was five-eighth: what in Britain would be called a stand-off half. I had just enough speed and agility to tempt myself into trouble, but not enough of either to get out of it. My short career was effectively finished in a game against Manly, whose two enormous breakaways, like the clashing rocks of mythology, hit me from different directions while I was wondering what to do with the ball. Semiconscious and feeling like an old car after it has been compressed into a block of scrap metal, I scored against my own side on the subsequent move and thus acquired the tag 'Wrong Way' James.

But at least I was able to have 'Third Grade Football 1956' embroidered in blue silk under the school badge on the breast pocket of my maroon blazer. Senior boys were encouraged thus to emblazon their achievements. My paltry single line of glory looked insignificant enough on its own and ludicrous beside the listed battle honours of the true sporting stars, which extended below their pockets onto the blazer itself. 'First Grade Football 1954. First Grade Football 1955. First Grade Football 1956. CHS Swimming 1952. CHS Swimming 1953 . . .' My lost companion Carnaby had a block of blue print on his blazer that looked, from a distance, like a page of heroic couplets. As for the Captain of the School, Leslie Halyard, it was lucky he was seven feet tall, since his credits went on and on like the titles of an epic movie.

The blazer was an important item of equipment. I bought mine after I was elected one of the school's eighteen prefects. I came in at number seventeen on the poll, one ahead of the school bell-ringer. Without the Third Grade football credit I never would have made it, and would thus never have enjoyed the heady privilege of supervising detention or of booking other boys for running in the playground. Admission to the rank of prefect was my sole latter-day school success. In other respects I might as well not have come to school at all. Indeed most of my clothes looked as if they had already left. By this time young men's fashions were reflecting the influence of *Rock Around the Clock* and *Don't Knock the Rock*. Another influence was the lingering impact of the bodgie era, which had occupied the immediately preceding years. The bodgies had favoured a drape-shape rather like the British Teddy-boys, with shoes the size of Volkswagens and a heavily built-up hairstyle razored square across the neck. The American tennis manager Jack Kramer also played an important part in shaping our appearance, even though his palpable influence was confined to the apex of the head. His flat-top haircut was faithfully reflected by what occurred on top of our own craniums, where each hair rose vertically to the level of a single, imaginary horizontal plane and then stopped dead. Even Halyard, normally conservative in his attire, turned up one day with the top of his head looking as if it had been put through a bandsaw. Griffiths set up a barber shop in the prefects' room and gave us his skilled attention, checking the results with a T-square. Well greased with Brylcreem, the side panels of our haircuts were left to grow long and be swept back with an octagonal, many-spiked plastic rake which looked like the inside of an Iron Maiden for butterflies. At the back, above the straight-as-a-die bottom line, a muted duck's arse effect occurred, further echoing the just-vanished bodgie ideal and directly presaging the incoming cultural onslaught of *77 Sunset Strip*, among the first programmes to be shown on Australian television. Continuing to read downwards, we come to the drape-shape jacket. The emphasis was on heavily padded shoulders and a waistless taper towards a hemline on the lower thighs. Cut to my personal specifications, the drape of my own jacket was so tastefully judged that you had to look for several seconds before noticing how a supernumerary set of shoulders, sloping at a steeper angle, started where the real ones ended. Shirt and tie were something assertive from a shop near Museum station called Scottish Tailoring, the pink, cerise or Mitchell Blue shirt flecked with white and the multi-banded iridescent slub tie cut square at the bottom like a decapitated coral snake. Scottish

Tailoring also supplied the peg-top bottle-green slacks with the fourteen-inch cuffs and the personalized fobs. Socks were usually chosen in some contrasting colour to the shirt. I favoured mauve socks myself, since they interposed an arresting bravura passage between the bottle-green cuffs and the quilt-top ox-blood shoes with the half-inch-thick crêpe soles. Moving, the shoes made a noise like cowpats at the moment of impact. Stationary, they allowed their occupant to lean over at any angle. You will understand that I am describing a representative outfit for day wear. In the evening I dressed up. Somewhere else, in the parallel universe inhabited by the Australian equivalent of the middle class, boys of my age must have been learning to feel at ease with their advantages. Doubtless I would have found theirs a world of stultifying conventionality, had I known it. But I never knew it. The essence of a class system is not that the privileged are conscious of their privileges, but that the deprived are conscious of their deprivation. Deprived I never felt. I had neither the insight nor the power of observation to realize that there might be another breed who recognized each other simply by the untroubled, unquestioning way they shared good manners, well-cut clothes and shoes that never wore out. I didn't feel disadvantaged. I just felt lost. Conforming desperately with my nonconformist outward show, inwardly I could find nobody to identify with – certainly not Marlon Brando in *The Wild One* or James Dean in *Rebel Without a Cause*. The inarticulacy of those two heroes would have been a blessed retreat. Instead I was the captive of my fluent tongue. The effort of being continuously diverting left me limp. I never doubted that those were the only terms on which I would ever be accepted.

Close friends would probably have been there had I really wanted them. But that would have taken time from the daily task of playing to the gallery. To that, the only alternative I could ever countenance was solitude. Very occasionally I went out with Gary on the pillion of the BSA 500, but by now the refurbished one-lunger was disturbingly fast. Even in top gear the separate ignition

strokes were still audible, but the vacuum behind me swelled my
shirt out like a spinnaker, the airstream was hard on the eyes and
when we heeled over in the corners I thought the speeding asphalt
was coming up to hit me in the ear. Eventually he sold the 500
and bought a BSA 350 OHV which he started to adapt for racing.
No matter what he did with it, it would never be as quick as
the AJS 7Rs that dominated its class, but it was still a demanding
machine with expensive tastes. There was no longer much room in
his life for me.

My mother and I still went to every change of programme at
both Ramsgate and Rockdale Odeons, so we were seeing at least
four movies a week. She sat there dutifully through the war films,
even though she despised most of them. She got really angry at
John Wayne in *Sands of Iwo Jima*. Musicals she couldn't take, but
she still sat there, generously keeping me company while I envied
Gene Kelly and doted on Cyd Charisse. She even sat still for Betty
Hutton, though she would rather have had her teeth drilled. In fact
the only film she ever walked out of was *Hot Blood*, an epic of
gypsy life in which Cornel Wilde and Jane Russell stared significantly at each other through the flickering light of the campfire,
very occasionally raising their arms above their heads as if to check
up on the current state of their own armpits, although it turned
out that they were only getting ready to dance. My mother and I
quarrelled frequently but we reached a comforting unanimity on
such matters as what constituted a lousy picture. She could be very
funny about poor Mario Lanza. She took her revenge over antipa-
thetic film stars by getting their names wrong. Muttering imprecations at Dolores Day and Susan Hollywood, she was good company
as we walked home through the night along Rocky Point Road. For
years the mere mention of Lizabeth Scott, renamed Elspeth Scott,
was enough to send us both into hysterics. I wish our closeness
could have been at least partly due to a conscious effort from me.
On the contrary, it was only our apartness that was fuelled by my
will. She knew that I was doing badly in my last years at high

school. I knew she was right, but didn't want to admit that I had made a mistake. When we clashed, the talk and the tears went on for hours, leaving both of us exhausted.

So at most it was a family of two, except for Christmas, when we always went to visit Aunt Dot in Jannali. Aunt Dot laid on a Christmas tree and an enormous Christmas dinner, eaten as usual at noon on Christmas day. The fatted calf scarcely ranked among the hors d'oeuvres. Everything was still as scalding hot as the day Grandpa spat the zac. The same trifles, plum puddings and lemon-meringue pies. Decorated with cotton-wool snow, brittle globular doodads and strings of tinsel, the tree shed dry green needles and presents for me. Another highlight of the trip was a visit around the corner to some distant relatives called the Sturrocks. The size of troglodytes and older than the hills, they crouched in the stygian depths of their weatherboard house and croaked greetings. All their lives they had gone on putting on clothes without ever taking them off. I believe they were spontaneously combustible, like those people in Dickens. The whole of Christmas was a solemn ritual but my mother and my aunt needed to be close even when they got on badly. Their brothers had never been much use to them, so they supported and comforted each other as their losses mounted. I would have been proud of both of them if I had had any sense. Lacking that, I withdrew into myself and counted the hours until I could be alone again.

At school and church I got by as an entertainer, but it was a solitary's way of being gregarious. I was never really at ease in company. Nowadays I am at last blessed with friends so close that I don't even feel the need to try, but at the time I am talking about such friendships belonged to other people. I observed them enviously from a distance. It was only in my own company that I could switch off the act. Until the Glaciarium closed down I used to go skating alone there twice a week all through the winter, on Wednesday afternoon after school and for two sessions on Saturday. I bought a second-hand pair of Puckmaster ice-hockey skates. They were a typically bad buy, although not as bad as the football boots that were three sizes too big and finished my Boys' Brigade soccer career before it began, since I had to run some distance before the boots started to move. The hockey skates were merely clapped out in the heels and soles, so that that the screws pulled out and the blades parted company from the boots at critical moments. But on the days when my skates stayed together I was perfectly content, circulating endlessly while ogling that prettiest of all sights, the line formed by the behind and upper thigh of a girl skater. I never went to classes and could perform no tricks more complicated than a 'three', but I had a flash turn of speed. During the fast skating periods I could run quickly enough in the turns to lay my inside hand on the ice – the surest way of pleasing the crowd, especially if another skater removed your fingers. As usual, I was trying hard to look good, but there were also moments of genuine, monastic solitude. Talking contentedly to myself I would circle with the crowd, zigzagging to hold my speed down and tucking one hand inside my windbreaker, like Napoleon. Perhaps Napoleon found out that he had chicken pox the same way I did. It was a hot day outside, the ice was covered with an inch of slush, there were thousands of people jamming the rink, the loudspeakers were playing 'Don't Let the Stars Get In Your Eyes' and I discovered I had a little bubble on my stomach. Two little bubbles. Scores of little bubbles. I left immediately, guilty with the realization that I had infected the whole Glaciarium. It closed soon after, probably as a direct result. Since there was no other ice rink nearer than San Francisco, I hung up my skates.

But there was also my bicycle. Simultaneously with my first long trousers had arrived a scarlet 28-inch-frame Speedwell to replace the old brown 26-inch-frame rattletrap on which I used to tilt quixotically with the privet hedges. The frame of the new bike was not fully tapered but with my eyes half closed I could almost call it a racing bike, especially after I had it equipped with white-wall tyres and three-speed Sturmey-Archer hub gears. At the beginning the saddle was flush with the crossbar. By the time of my final year in school the saddle was extended to its full height.

I had given the bike's appointments a lot of thought. The gear-change trigger was placed next to one of the brake levers at the end of the ram's horn handlebars, so that changing down was like firing a gun, while all I had to do to change up was flex my knuckle. Impressively clad in striped T-shirt, sandshoes and khaki shorts with rolled-up legs, I rode many miles every weekend. I could be at Mascot aerodrome in a few minutes, at the George's River bridge in half an hour. Sometimes I rode all the way to the National Park, just so that I could coast down Artillery Hill. Boys got killed trying that: it was a long, long hill. The idea was to go down without ever touching the brakes and at the end to go streaking across the dam without any change in the stoic expression. No expression could have been more stoic than mine. The speed of the airstream was enough to distort my features until they looked like what happened to the rocket crew in *Destination Moon*, but underneath I was still heroically stoic. It was an important test, which I passed, although typically I was unable to do so without posing.

So I got used to travelling alone. It was hard on my mother, who earlier on had always been good at setting up interesting trips. She would sort out the details of trains, buses and boats, so that without effort I would find myself beside her watching the aborigines diving for coins at La Perouse, or howling along through the latticed girders of the Hawkesbury River bridge in the Newcastle Flyer. On the boat to Bundeena she got seats for us in the prow so that I could lean daringly over and watch the porpoises as they appeared, disappeared and reappeared in our bow-wave, sinking to spin around each other and rising in quick succession to blow a squirt of aerated water that sprinkled your delighted face like angel spit. Now *there* was a gang worth joining. My mother told me that there was nothing in the sea, not even sharks, that could hurt them, and that there was nothing they wanted to hurt. Those were the days when she could still tell me things. The breeze caught her hair and pulled it back. She looked like Garbo in *Anna Christie*. When the water grew shallow enough for the sand to be clearly visible the porpoises peeled away and left us together.

But now I knew it all and couldn't bear to be told, not even by myself. I shouted down my own conscience when it tried to inform me that I was well on the way to securing a Leaving Certificate which would scarcely rank as a dishonourable discharge. Even English had gone completely sour on me. I had my name down to take the English Honours paper. Big joke. I was fully qualified to answer anything that might be asked about Erle Stanley Gardner or Leslie Charteris, but beyond that I was perfectly clueless. None of the dozen books a week I had been taking out of the local public library had anything to do with literature. Nor was the teacher assigned to the Honours class likely to spot the discrepancy between my knowledge and the tests about to be made of it. He was, in the first place, a librarian. He was, in the second place, geriatric. He might have been Mary Luke's older brother. Where Mary started every lesson with instructions on how to make a Bunsen burner, Dewey – short for Dewey Decimal System – always began by showing you how to open a new book from the centre so that reading it would not distort the spine. The book's spine, not yours. He was probably sound on that one subject but on anything else he was a dead loss. While he burbled aimlessly for his allotted hour, I spent the time memorizing all the parts of the Moto Guzzi V-8 racing motorcycle engine. But I was already well aware that not even so prodigious a feat of memory would do me any good. It was the older boys, the ones who could do the maths, who would go on to design and construct the beautiful machines. While I read about cars, they were already buying them, taking them apart, putting them back together and driving them around. On the other hand, I was no longer any good at English either.

I entered the examination hall with the same feelings the RAAF pilots must have had when they flew Brewster Buffaloes into action against the Japanese – underpowered, outgunned, fearful and ashamed. I left the examination hall fondly recalling how well I had felt going in. The mathematics papers I had expected to find incomprehensible, but it was unmanning to find the English Honours paper equally opaque. It was full of questions about

people I had never heard of. Shakespeare's name I recognized
almost instantly, but who was George Eliot? What had he written?
I could do none of it. Simpler than going home would have been
to catch a tram to the Gap and jump off. I spent weeks reassuring
my mother that everything would be all right, while simultaneously
indicating that if everything turned out not to be all right it would
be no true measure of my real ability or future prospects. But
when the results appeared in the *Herald* the bluff was over. I got
an A and five Bs. The A was in English: it meant that I had failed
my Honours paper outright but had been above average in the
ordinary paper. Since the average mark for the ordinary English
paper had been set to coincide with the linguistic attainments of
Ginger Meggs this did not count for much. The five Bs meant that
I had wasted my time for a lustrum each in five different mathematical subjects – a total of twenty-five man-years straight down
the drain. About all that I had managed to achieve was matricula-
tion. It sounded like micturition and meant even less. Practically
anybody could matriculate. But you needed several more As than I
had achieved if you were to get a Commonwealth Scholarship, and
without one of those there was not much hope of acquiring a
university education. I was a total failure.

There was no longer any hope of dissuading my mother from
the conviction that she had been right all along. Even in the dust
and flame of the debacle, it was obvious that English had been my
best subject, or at any rate my least worst. In the mathematical
subjects which had been supposed to further my engineering career
I had scored almost nothing. I fought back with all the petulant
fervour of one who knows that he is in the wrong. In my heart I
had long known that the other boys would be the engineers. But
where did that leave me? What was the thing I was supposed to do,
now that it was proved I could do nothing else?

At this point, like the Fairy Godmother, the Repatriation
Commission stepped in. The Australian government never got
around to doing very much for war widows, but in a weak moment
it had developed a soft spot for war orphans, who could claim a

free university education as long as they matriculated. Far from having to meet Commonwealth Scholarship standards, they needed only to obtain the number and quality of passes that might be appropriate for an apprentice bottle-washer. By this absorbent criterion, I was in. All I had to do was apply. Even then I almost managed to persuade myself that I wanted to go to the University of Technology. If I had prevailed in this wish my mother would undoubtedly have ended it all under the wheels of a trolleybus. Luckily the Repat. wasn't having any. Sydney University it had to be. They advised an Arts course. Since I thought this meant drawing, at which I had always been rather good, I signed on the dotted line.

In retrospect it seems incredible even to me that I had come so far and remained so ignorant. It was not just that I was nowhere compared with an English sixth-former or an American prep-school graduate. I was nowhere compared even with my fellow Hurstville alumni who had gone to Sydney High. When I met Elstub on the train he was reading *The Age of Anxiety* and I was reading *Diving to Adventure*. Knowing nothing, I scarcely suspected what I was missing. Barely realizing what a university was, I looked forward to it as something vague on an indeterminate horizon. The immediate task was to survive as an office boy in the L. J. Hooker organization, my first proper job. In my senior high-school years I had tried several different jobs during the school holidays. The most disastrous was as a shop assistant in Coles, where I rapidly discovered that I was incapable of dealing with impatient customers without becoming flustered. Merely to discover that the anodized aluminium tray I was supposed to wrap was wider than the wrapping paper was enough to set me darting about distractedly in search of wider paper or a narrower anodized aluminium tray. In just such a frenzy I ran into a display stand on which were carefully arranged hundreds of cut-glass bowls, dishes and plates. The stuff proved to be amazingly durable, which raised questions about the composition of the glass. Instead of shattering, it bounced. But it bounced everywhere, and before the last piece had stopped rolling

I was on my way home. I had a similar job in Herb Horsfield's Hobby House, but rather than sell wind-up toys to wind-up customers I retreated into the toilet and read *The Caine Mutiny*. When Herb finally realized that he was making no sales at all when I was in charge he reluctantly opened discussions about terms of separation. He quite liked me, which was foolish of him in the circumstances.

L. J. Hooker's was a bigger thing all round. By this time my mother was in despair of my ever accomplishing anything. She had no idea what a university Arts course might be but she had every reason to suppose that I would make a hash of it. L. J. Hooker's, on the other hand, was the fastest-growing real-estate firm in Australia. If I applied myself I might work my way up. If only to blunt the edge of the disappointment in her eyes, I resolved to knuckle down. In the three months before university started, I would prove myself as an office boy to myself, my mother and the world.

The main office of L. J. Hooker's was situated in Martin Place, just near the Cenotaph. I got off the train at Wynyard every morning, walked to the building, descended to the basement, hung up my coat, picked up my scissors and applied myself to the thrilling task of cutting out all the L. J. Hooker classified ads in that day's *Herald*. It took most of the morning. The rest of the day I pasted them into a big book. At set intervals I also delivered mail all around the building, thereby giving myself the opportunity to die of love for the boss's secretary, a tall, ravishingly voluptuous girl called Miss Wiper. Every day, delivering the mail to her, I would greet her with a suave one-liner gleaming from the polish of twenty-four hours' sleepless rehearsal. 'Hi, patootie,' I would pipe casually, 'how goes it?' Her answering smile invariably floored me completely. I would enter her office looking as relaxed as Ronald Colman – if you can imagine Ronald Colman wearing quilted shoes the size of small cars – and leave it crawling and sobbing. It seemed to me at such moments that my love was being answered. Actually, I now realize, something more interesting was happening. A kind woman was enjoying, mischievously but without malice, the spectacle of awkward young manhood searching for a voice and manner. Where is she now? What lucky man did she marry?

But love for Miss Wiper is an insufficient explanation for how thoroughly I became alienated from the task. If I had been blessed with a gift for self-knowledge, I would have clearly recognized myself to be unemployable. As it was, this and many other attempts had to run their disastrous course before I at last learned that I am good for what I am good for and for nothing else. It was only by an accident of timing that I was able to resign from Hooker's before I got the boot. Every Friday after work I had to take the mail – which was all contained in a special large envelope – across Martin Place to the GPO and drop it in the slot. Then I had to take another large envelope full of copy for the weekend's classified advertising around the corner to the *Herald* building and leave it at the desk. On the Friday before the week I was due to leave, I paid both these calls, hopped on the train at Wynyard and was off to Kogarah for the usual weekend of quarrels, movies and long, lonely bike rides. Since we had no telephone, I did not have to answer for my latest achievement until Monday morning, when I got to the office and found a note on my desk from Miss Wiper asking if I could come up and see her as soon as it might be convenient.

Pausing only to comb my hair for half an hour, I translated myself to her office, the first lines of an off-hand speech already vibrant on my lips. She forestalled me with the information that it was L.J.H. – meaning Mr Hooker himself – who was requesting my presence. I had barely time to die the first nine hundred of a thousand deaths before I was in the great man's office and face to face with him across a desk which I at first thought was tapered at the sides, until I realized it was so big that my stunned vision was being struck by the perspective. There was nothing on top of the desk except L.J.H.'s folded hands and two empty envelopes. 'The famous Mr James, isn't it?' enquired L.J.H. This was the time to tell him that I was not the famous Mr James at all, but was in fact Group Captain the Baron Waldemar Incognito of the Moldavian

Secret Service on a sensitive diplomatic mission which, alas, demanded that I should leave immediately by the nearest window. Unfortunately the words would not come, partly because my tongue had spot-welded itself to the roof of my mouth. 'Luckily the GPO and the *Herald* both got on to us while there was still time,' L.J.H. reassured me. 'A pity, in one way. You realize our weekend classified advertising involves several hundred thousand pounds' worth of business. It would have been the biggest mistake any office boy had ever made anywhere in the world. You would have been in Ripley.' By Ripley L.J.H. meant a newspaper feature called *Believe It or Not*, in which the readers were asked to marvel at such phenomena as a man who had cut down a gum tree with his teeth, or an office boy who had put half a million pounds' worth of classified advertisements through the wrong hole.

L.J.H. stood up. He looked very large. He also, I was pathetically relieved to note, looked very kind. He had his hand stuck out. At first I thought he was inviting me to read his palm, but then I realized he was saying goodbye. 'Something tells me that we'll be hearing more from you one day. Perhaps in some other line of work. You're going to the University, I believe.' It was a statement, not a question, but it gave me a chance to say something. 'Nyengh.' L.J.H. generously chose to ignore this further evidence that he was dealing with a Venusian, just as he had chosen to ignore the distilled water dripping from my hand. 'It's a good life. You'll find yourself there.' I was on my way out, going backwards. The oak door was shut. I was alone with Miss Wiper. Silently she offered me a Mintie.

13. LET US REJOICE, THEREFORE

Freshers and freshettes arrived at the university a week before full term in order to be inducted into the academic life by means of lectures, displays, film shows and theatrical events. The period was known as Orientation Week, a title which confused me, since I failed to see why the Far East should be involved. The university motto was *Sidere mens eadem mutato*, which loosely translated means 'Sydney University is really Oxford or Cambridge laterally displaced approximately twelve thousand miles.' In fact the differences were enormous. For one thing, there were few colleges: the overwhelming majority of students arrived in the morning and left in the evening. In the Arts course you could read several subjects, rather like the American system. The way to pass exams was to reproduce the lectures. Personal supervision – the heart of the Oxbridge system – scarcely existed. There was a Union for debates and a certain amount of strained singing in which *Gaudeamus igitur* featured prominently, but on the whole the emphasis was on pushing forward to get one's degree. With careers as lawyers or upper-echelon schoolteachers in mind, the Arts students were even more dedicated to exam-passing than anyone else. There was a day shift and a night shift, both toiling away nervelessly towards their nine passes. It took some of them the maximum allowable nine years, but they all got there. Nobody who wanted to pass ever failed, not even the beautiful, elegantly groomed, ineffably dumb girls from Frensham who had been sent along to acquire some elementary culture before resuming their inexorable progress towards marriage with a grazier. Any real originality of mind or behaviour was confined to the astrophysics department or the medical school, which both ranked high in world standing. The huge Arts faculty placed as little emphasis on the human imagination as was consistent with the study of its products.

Even for Australia, the late 1950s were an unusually apolitical, conformist period. Nevertheless a certain amount of eccentricity took place. There were about two dozen illuminati who dominated the student newspaper *honi soit*, edited and contributed to the magazines *Hermes* and *Arna* and produced, directed and acted in plays put on by SUDS (the Dramatic Society) and Players (the other dramatic society). Making a career out of failing first-year Arts on an annual basis, this coherent little group were hard to miss during Orientation Week, since they were continually trotting up and down Science Road in order to take turns manning the publicity booths relating to their various activities. The booth for *honi soit* was called the Flying Saucer, since it was a circular plywood creation with a pointed roof. It was only about six feet in diameter but at the moment of my arrival it was crammed with these exotic creatures, the like of which I had never seen. Nor, I think, had they seen anything quite like me. I had turned up in my school blazer, but in order to indicate that I was a man of parts I had pinned my Presbyterian Fellowship badge to the lapel, alongside the Boys' Brigade badge in my buttonhole. A brown briefcase contained sandwiches. My haircut looked like an aircraft carrier for flies.

But at worst they were seeing an extreme example of a known type, the clueless fresher. I, on the other hand, was seeing something I could not even compare with other examples of itself. I hadn't known that people were allowed to look like this. The women had long, stringy black hair, heavy eye make-up and smoked cigarettes no hands. The men smoked their cigarettes in long holders. They affected flannel shirts, corduroy trousers and the kind of long-nosed desert boots which I was subsequently informed were called brothel-creepers. During this first encounter I could see nothing of these people below waist level, since only their upper works showed above the counter of the Flying Saucer.

But their tightly packed heads, arms and torsos were sufficiently extraterrestrial to leave me numb with awe. 'My God,' cried the shortest of the men, 'it's a Christian! Come and work for *honi soit*. We need a broad spectrum of opinion. You could offset the influence of Wanda here. She's a witch.' The girl referred to as Wanda coughed her assent, projecting a small puff of ash. 'My name is Spencer,' said the same short man again. He had jug ears, horn-rimmed glasses and a crew cut. 'Sign here and report for duty at the office tomorrow morning. It's around that corner. A sort of hut arrangement in Early Permanent Temporary. Here is a sample copy of the paper. Those badges are distorting the shape of what would be a perfectly good jacket, if it were a different colour and cut.'

Threading my way in a daze through the other booths, a good quarter of which were magically staffed by the same raggle-taggle team I had just met in the Flying Saucer, I entered the Union building, mechanically bought a tie dotted with the University crest and sat down in the reading room to look at my sample copy of *honi soit*. Half of it seemed to be written by Spencer. There was a short story by him of which I could make little and some poems of which I could make even less. One of the poems was about Rimbaud's cigar. Who was Rimbaud? Yet in another way I saw the point instantly. The vividness of the language was extraordinary. Even when crammed into meticulously symmetrical verse forms every sentence sounded like speech. I can't say that my future course was set there and then, but neither can I say that it wasn't. I was so excited that my badges rattled. There were sparks coming off my lapel.

Later that day I attended the Sex Lecture and laughed knowingly along with all the other nervous virgins. I joined both the Film Group and the Film Society, though I had no idea how they differed. I joined almost everything. I wondered where I could buy a pair of brothel-creepers. Every time it all became too much I retreated to my bolt-hole in the Union reading room and looked at *honi soit* again. The cartoons were amazingly good. They were signed 'Huggins'. Everybody who counted seemed to have only one name. Every other leather chair in the reading room was similarly occupied by a freshman looking, I was relieved to note, not much more at ease than myself. Indeed few could smoke as confidently as I, although everyone was trying. It was like a bush fire in there.

I headed for home bamboozled with smoke and strange, unfocused dreams. At tea I blew smoke into my mother's face and explained that at University one was expected to join in a wide range of extracurricular activities in order to broaden one's outlook. I sketched reassuring verbal pictures of how I would explore caves with the Speleological Society and jump with the Parachute Club. My mother doubtless had the look of someone whose troubles are only just beginning, but my mouth was too far open for my eyes to notice anything.

Next day I turned up at the *honi soit* office bright and early, several times tripping adroitly on the short flight of steps. I was wearing my new brothel-creepers, bought on the way up the hill from Central Station. My old ox-blood quilt-tops were in my briefcase. I had chosen a pair of brothel-creepers with very long toes. They must have looked, to the independent observer, rather like the footwear of a peculiarly unsubtle clown. Certainly it was hard to climb stairs in them without turning sideways, so my arrival in the office proper was somewhat crablike. The Flying Saucer crew were all in there, plus a few more I was seeing for the first time. Wanda was still smoking no hands. Spencer was sitting at a typewriter. A tall man looking like an illustration of a kindly young history master in an English public school was standing beside him.

'Good morning,' said Spencer without ceasing to type. 'This is Keith Cameron.' The tall man said, 'How do you do. Sandwich?' 'You aren't expected to take one,' said Spencer. 'Cameron is merely being polite. Wanda you already know. The man in the suit is John Bottomley.' Bottomley was conservatively tailored for the year 1908. He wore spats. 'The man in the other suit is Jim Howie.' Howie was dressed and groomed for the grouse moors. 'Wanda will show you how to edit copy. Meanwhile Cameron and I will get on with this diverting lampoon for the next issue. On behalf of us all Howie and Bottomley are hatching a plot to unseat the editor, who is an idiot. For a blessing he is not present. A no-confidence motion concerning the editorship will be put at a special meeting in the Wallace Theatre this afternoon at three o'clock. Here is Maurice Grogan.'

Grogan swung into the office by one hand, which was reverse-gripped around the upper door-frame. He wore nothing on his superbly muscular body except a Speedo the size of a G-string, a pair of the kind of sandals known as Hong Kong thongs and a beard. He jumped up on a desk and crouched, gibbering and snickering. Nobody seemed to notice. I sedulously copied every-body else's indifference while Wanda showed me how to sub-edit the readers' letters. To do this she had to use her hands – my first evidence that they were not paralysed. When she pointed things out she did not always point to the right place because her eyes were screwed up. Ash fell from her cigarette, which she allowed to grow remarkably short during the course of her lesson. I was afraid her face would catch fire. Meanwhile the conspirators conspired and the creators created, both colloquies being punctuated by low growls and high-pitched squeals from Grogan. As they worked, Cameron and Spencer kept up an exchange of allusive wit that I found at once daunting and exhilarating. Spencer called something Firbankian. Who, what or where was Firbankian? I was lost, yet not in the usual way of feeling that I ought to be somewhere else. Somehow I knew that I was in exactly the right spot.

'Shall we lunch at Manning or the Forest Lodge?' asked Spencer. 'Let's remember,' said Cameron, 'the importance of remaining sober.' 'Not as important as having a drink,' said Bottomley. 'And besides, we'll never get the fool out anyway. A gesture is the most we can hope to achieve.' With me attached, the whole caravan moved across Parramatta Road, up a flight of steps and along the street to a pub called the Forest Lodge, which during opening hours was the daytime headquarters of the artistic set. We all trooped through the back gate while Grogan swarmed over the wall. Again nobody took any notice. I was later to learn that Grogan was Spencer's steady date. Spencer was bisexual but least unhappy with Grogan. The same applied to Grogan vis-à-vis Spencer. For a long time I was incapable of grasping any of these facts, being under the impression that homosexuality was some kind of rare disease. I am glad to say that incomprehension gave way to tolerance without any intervening period of bigotry. But enlightenment lay far in the future, and for the time being I was as innocent as Queen Victoria when young.

As in all Australian pubs at the time, the beer came in two kinds, New and Old. New was made yesterday and Old was made the day before. I asked for a schooner of New, manfully not betraying the fact that it was the second drink of my life. It differed from the first drink in that I was able to sip it without gagging. It still tasted like camel's pee. I closed my eyes so that nobody would notice they were crossed. But my ears were functioning perfectly. They had never had so much to listen to. The brain between them could process only the odd scrap of the information that was streaming in through the aural receptors. I had never heard such conversation. What kind of car, I wondered, was a Ford Madox Ford? What sort of conflict was an Evelyn War? At the mention of *Decline and Fall*, I advanced the name of Gibbon. Cameron gently explained that the book in question was written by the aforesaid War, spelt Waugh. Had I not read anything by him? Who was my idea of a good modern novelist? I said Nicholas Monsarrat. There were snorts all round at this. All present snorted audibly. Wanda snorted visibly. Spencer cast his eyes to the sky. But Cameron saved my face by insisting that there were good reasons for admiring Monsarrat, especially in his less famous works such as *HMS Marlborough Will Enter Harbour*. I would find, however, Cameron assured me, that Waugh's early novels were unbeatable for comic invention. 'How can you talk about Waugh when I'm reading Firbank?' Spencer asked a cloud. 'Here's Huggins.'

Through the gate walked the most artistic-looking young man

I had ever seen in my two days' experience of artistic young men. He was all pale suede and corduroy. The ends of a loosely knit scarf dangled almost to the ground. He had a folio under his arm. Surrounding a face so handsome it was like a cartoon, his hair was blond and abundant. He was smoking a cigarette about two feet long. Within seconds he was seated, sipping at a beer glass held in one hand while he sketched with the other. He did a group sketch of everybody present. I was staggered – by the speed of his hand, by the quality of what it produced, and by the fact that I was included in the result, which I was allowed to keep. That night I pasted it onto my wall at home, airily explaining to my mother that it was the work of my friend Huggins, whom I knew quite well, since he was a close acquaintance of mine, and had in fact sat beside me during the vitally important meeting in which the editor of *honi soit* had retained his position only by a hair's breadth. Actually, I now realize, any condemnation emanating from my new acquaintances had the effect of vociferous advocacy, just as anything they favoured was automatically doomed. Spencer's speech had clinched the issue. He mentioned Cocteau, Kleist and Lord Alfred Douglas. The chairman imposed a gag and put the motion to a vote. It was lost by five hundred and sixty votes to eight. I was one of the eight.

From that day my university career proceeded on two separate paths, one of them curricular and the other not. In my new desert boots, but still retaining my Fellowship badge, I attended lectures in my four first-year subjects, English I, Modern History I, Psychology I and Anthropology I. One among hundreds, I sat taking elaborate notes. I see no reason to mock myself in retrospect for so slavishly writing everything down: nearly all of it was news to me, and some of it was to prove permanently useful. The lectures on phonetics, for example, were a painless way for a writer to pick up essential knowledge about what sounds really rhyme even when they look as if they don't, and what sounds really don't rhyme even when they look as if they do. Twenty years later I am still drawing on that knowledge every day. Nor was I in any position to scorn

elementary lectures on the time shift in *A Passage to India*, since
I was not yet fully divested of the impression that E. M. Forster's
principal creation had been Horatio Hornblower. As for *A Portrait
of the Artist as a Young Man*, I certainly needed help there, having
been only dimly aware that Ireland was a Catholic country.

Modern History helped to make me less clueless on such points.
The English component of the History course was occupied mainly
with Tudor constitutional documents. To the suitably unprepared
student it could not have been duller. But the European side of
things introduced me to the Anabaptists, the Medici, the Habsburgs
and a charming group of bankers called the Fuggers. Even here,
though, I had trouble establishing a perspective. What had been so
wonderful about the Renaissance? Why had Burckhardt bothered
even to the extent of being wrong about it? But my pen raced on,
unhampered by the mind's doubts. I didn't even know enough to
know that what I now knew meant nothing without the knowledge
that was meant to go around it.

Anthropology lectures were full of references to Evans-Pritchard,
Radcliffe-Brown and Margaret Mead. The set books had titles like
Growing Up in New Guinea, *Structure and Function in Primitive
Pago-Pago* and *Having It Off In Hawaii*. Every time evolution got
a mention, the girls in the audience who belonged to Sancta
Sophia College would put a conscience-saving mark at the top of
the page and discreetly cross themselves. Since they ran to angora
twin-sets, this last move would involve a gentle but tangible-
looking self-inflicted pressure on their cosily enclosed bosoms,
which in several cases were of notable size and shape. Watching
one especially pretty Catholic girl called Noeleen Syms thus deli-
cately caressing her own breasts, I sucked so thoughtfully on my
biro that I was favoured with a sudden, solid mouthful of black
ink. For the next week I had lips like a silent-movie star and teeth
like the Mikado.

Psychology was taught by a faculty composed exclusively of
mechanists, behaviourists and logical-positivists. They would have
made Pavlov sound like a mystic had he been foolish enough to

show up. He must have heard about how boring they were, since he never appeared, but it was not for want of having his name invoked. The whole faculty salivated en masse at the mere mention of him. As so often happens, dogmatic contempt for the very idea of the human soul was accompanied by limitless belief in the quantifiability of human personality. On the one hand we were informed that there was no ghost in the machine. On the other we were taught how to administer tests which would measure whether children were well adjusted. But quite a lot of solid information was embedded in the pulp. Since there was nothing I did not write down and memorize, the real information was still there years later, when all the theoretical blubber surrounding it had rotted away. A synapse, after all, remains a synapse, even after some clod has tried to convince you that Michelangelo's talent can be explained in terms of the number and intensity of electrical impulses travelling across it. Or do I mean a ganglion?

Thus I applied myself. At that time a genuinely important man, Professor John Anderson, was head of the Philosophy Faculty and still delivering his famous lectures on logic to first-year classes, but typically I had failed to set my name down for the only subject that might have stimulated a mental component more intricate than mere memory. As it was, I did not sustain the full impact of Anderson's realism until some years later. For the time being it was taxing enough to absorb elementary information about palatal fricatives, gametes, Dyak kinship patterns and the theological significance of Zwingli. Walled in behind a stack of books with titles like *We of the Wee-Wee* and *Dropping Your Lunch in the Desert*, I sat at the back of the Wallace Theatre with a fairly steady set of companions. Most of them had already graduated out of school blazers into sports coats, but it was plain that in their case raffishness would go no further. Less square than the out-and-out exam-passers, they were still not bohemians. They were ex-GPS and lived in fashionable harbourside suburbs like Bellevue Hill and Rose Bay. Without exception they were on their way to becoming lawyers. For them, Arts was a couple of easy years before the real

work started. Some of them drove MG TCs. Their real life happened away from the university, but they talked about it while they
were there. Admiring their relaxation, I was glad to be in with
them and vaguely hoped that some of their ease would rub off on
me.

On the way to lectures, during lectures and after lectures they
all watched girls, awarding points for prettiness of face, size of
chest, etc. Twenty years later they are probably still talking the
same way and doing the same things. They were lucky enough to
get set in their ways early. I warmed to them because they knew
exactly what they were and liked being it. Their self-assurance,
I need hardly add, was no virtue in itself, and to admire it was
an admission of inadequacy on my part. Doubtless I would have
warmed to the Waffen-SS for the same reason. Luckily the group
in question happened to be harmless. Gilbert Bolt was the ringleader, mainly through being even less energetic than the rest of
them. Leading from behind was a technique I had not previously
encountered. Somehow, without lifting a finger, he made ordinary
things amusing. He looked half asleep most of the time. Raising an
eyebrow about a millimetre was his way of advising me to calm
down.

Perhaps the Bellevue Hill mob were my anchor to windward,
because simultaneously I was becoming more and more involved
with the aesthetes. Except for the Film Society, I soon came to have
no other extracurricular activity. Nor did I last long as an active
member of the Film Society. Their screenings took place at lunchtime in the Union Hall, a highly atmospheric neo-Gothic nightmare
of a place which was unforgivably pulled down a few years later.
Everybody was there. Members of the Film Society sat in the
minstrel gallery while the common herd sat in the hall proper.
Before the house lights dimmed an old 78 of Bunk Johnson and
George Lewis performing 'When the Saints Go Marching In' was
played over the public-address system. I was proud to be among
those in the gallery but it was fated that I should join the majority
below. There were two full-sized 35mm projectors. We manned

them with a crew of two, stripped to the waist because of the heat. I found it hard to keep the carbon arc burning at the right intensity. When the picture got dark, I overdid it with the readjustment, so that the picture got too bright. I never noticed a stoppage until the film melted. On the screen, Alan Ladd and Virginia Mayo would turn to stone and be suddenly overwhelmed by bubbling gravy. A junior member was supposed never to be left alone in the box but in practice the senior crew member was often outside in the gallery palpating his girlfriend.

If I had had help, the fourth reel of *Simba* would probably never have got away from me. The take-up reel fell off its spindle, leaving me a clear choice of shutting down the projector or else letting the film pile up on the floor. I chose the second course, unaware of just how much volume a reel of film occupies when unwound. When it was time for the next reel change, my senior colleague, whose name was Pratt and who was sitting outside in the gallery, retrieved his hand from his girlfriend's blouse and opened the door to the box. He was expecting to see me and the projectors. Instead he was confronted with a pulsing, writhing wall of celluloid. I was somewhere inside it. It was at least half his fault. But screening *Tales of Ugetsu* with its reels in the wrong order was entirely my responsibility, since I was in charge of film preparation that day. I suppose I marked the reels wrongly. Hardly anybody noticed the difference, but I realized that it was time to dismiss myself from the Film Society and join its public.

Anyway, I had started to begrudge any of my spare time that was not spent with the bohemians. The Union Revue would have been enough on its own to win my allegiance to their cause. By some act of folly Spencer and Cameron had been placed in charge of the revue for that year. They called it *Flying Saucers*. Between them they wrote all the scripts. They also appeared in most of the songs and sketches. The decor, by Huggins, was brilliant when you could see it. Spencer, however, had designed the lighting. Little would have been visible even if those Film Society members who were operating the dimmers had contrived to stay sober. There was great emphasis on dry ice, so that slow billows of mist crept from the stage into the auditorium, which gradually came to resemble a polar landscape in which people had been embedded up to the neck. Ultraviolet light made the actors' teeth glow green through the white fog. Instrumental music came from an electronic synthesizer played by Pratt. Vocal music was by Palestrina. There were at least two sketches about Virginia Woolf. A third sketch might have been about her, but was more probably about Gertrude Stein. Grogan played Alice B. Toklas, or it could have been Vita Sackville-West. Wanda was either in the cast or kept crossing the stage for some other reason. Bottomley and Howie, sharing the one pair of large trousers, purported to be a mutation. They mouthed abstract dialogue, partly as a forecast of how language might deteriorate in the aftermath of an atomic war, partly in deference to the fact that nobody had got around to actually writing the sketch. A tall, beautiful girl called Penelope White came on wearing a gown composed of shaving mirrors. She announced, in a voice like a chainsaw hitting granite, that her song had not been written yet, but that Spencer had asked her to recite a poem. She recited it. I subsequently learned that it was by John Crowe Ransom. During her recitative, Spencer stood on one leg in the background, softly tapping a gong.

Interval was longer than the first half, which in turn was longer than the second half, although it was hard to tell when that was over. The audience, except for myself and my companion, had left long before. My companion was a girl from Kogarah Presbyterian Church Fellowship called Robin Warne. Afterwards I took her home to Carlton, telling her, during the long train trip, that Spencer and Cameron believed in pitching their work at a level which would force the audience either to confess itself inadequate or else translate its prejudices into violence. I quoted Spencer to the effect that an audience should be challenged, not coddled. When Robin announced that she hadn't understood or enjoyed a single moment of the evening from start to finish, I countered with Spencer's favourite word: 'Precisely.'

She burst out laughing when I tried to kiss her and didn't speak to me the following Sunday, but I didn't notice. I was too busy planning that year's Kogarah Fellowship revue, which I called *Unidentified Flying Objects*. As producer and director I appointed myself sole scriptwriter and cast myself in every sketch. Lacking adequate supplies of dry ice, I set fire to some rags in a plastic bucket. Graham Truscott, decorated with a joke moustache of his own devising, was in charge of sound, which consisted of a jewel from my recently begun modern-jazz collection – an EP record featuring Maynard Ferguson and Clark Terry engaged in a long attempt to damage each other's hearing. I had tested this particular disc a few hundred times on my mother and could vouch for its challenging effect. As the trumpeters interminably wailed and shrieked, I improvised monologues in which such names as Ford Madox Ford and Ronald Firbank figured prominently. The audience stormed the exits.

That same week, the Fellowship newspaper, of which I was editor and leading contributor, was largely devoted to a long article extolling the virtues of atheism. I had cribbed this almost word for word from the preface to *Androcles and the Lion*, one of the set books for English I. Shaw had enchanted me with his rationalist blarney. It was fitting that my shallow faith should have been uprooted by a toy shovel. The Reverend C. Cummings Campbell asked me along for afternoon tea at the Manse. Still coughing from his evening at the one and only performance of *Unidentified Flying Objects* (handicapped by a pair of lungs which had been poisoned at Ypres, he had been among the last to fight his way out of the hall), he nevertheless managed to contain his anger. Instead of booting me immediately into the street, he began by gently suggesting that I might care to offload some of my more onerous responsibilities, such as the editorship of the Fellowship newspaper, until I had worked out of my system what was plainly 'the influence of that man Anderson'. As usual I was careful to resign a split second before being fired. I told him that I did indeed need time to think, and that perhaps it would be better if for the nonce I

were to absent myself altogether. He heaved what would have been
a sigh of relief if it had not turned into a coughing fit. My last
vision of all things Presbyterian was of the piece of sponge cake –
it had pink icing – which I had parked uneaten on the edge of my
saucer.

Showing my usual capacity to walk away without a qualm, I left
it all behind upon the instant: the bugles and the drums, the vaulting
horse and the oak pews, Christine Ballantine's eyes like a pleading
fawn and Mrs Pike's voice like a strangled fowl. I had no doubts
that I was through with it all for ever. My cocksureness must have
been terrible to behold. Night after night I reduced my mother to
tears with my intellectual arrogance. Copied sedulously from
Spencer, but potentiated by an insensitivity that was all my own,
my forensic style was as intransigent as Vyshinsky's. Ferociously
I attacked my mother's lingering, atavistic determination to go on
believing in something. If she didn't believe in anything specific,
I insisted, why couldn't she just believe in nothing? Triumphantly I
refuted her arguments, never recognizing that they were true feelings
and amounted to a deep intuition of the world, which in the long
run we must see to be purposeful if we are to live in it at all.

I suppose that first year at university was just about the most
ridiculous phase of my life. It was love again, of course, but this
time I was in love with all of them. I copied Spencer's walk, talk
and gestures. I copied the way he wrote. I copied the way Keith
Cameron read: Spencer, lost in the toils of a fully bisexual love life
and a chronic deficiency of funds, hardly ever read anything except
science fiction. I soon realized that his *pronunciamentos* on literature in general were based on the most evanescent acquaintance
with its individual products. But Cameron, who already had a BA
degree and was qualifying to begin an MA, had an impressive
private library of modern literature. I devoured it author by author.
Spencer had told me *Four Quartets* was the greatest thing written
in recent times. I practically memorized it, but was bewildered to
find that Spencer had switched his allegiance to Edith Sitwell.
Cameron was less capricious. His level head was the necessary

corrective to Spencer's influence. Huggins I admired for grace, ease, creative fertility and plethora of beautiful girlfriends. He was always promising to let me have one of them when he had finished with her, but somehow it never came about. This was lucky in a way, because I would scarcely have known how to behave. I had a girlfriend of my own, an Arts I student called Sally Vaughan: sweet, pretty, decent and intelligent. There was a lot of heavy petting going on but she was a Catholic, I was an idiot and there was nowhere to take her anyway. She lived with her parents in Mosman, across the harbour. I still went home every night, although later and later as the year wore on, especially after I had discovered in myself a liking for the effects produced by several schooners of New consumed one after the other.

In the Forest Lodge I drank with the Bellevue Hill mob and the aesthetes. With Spencer, Huggins, Grogan and Wanda (Cameron was a teetotaller) I visited my first King's Cross cafes and became acquainted with wine. There was more of the same stuff at Lorenzini's, a wine bar where the university writers made contact with the intelligentsia of the town. Lex Banning, the spastic poet, was often to be found there. But the place where all the half-worlds met was the Royal George Hotel, down in Pyrmont. The Royal George was the headquarters of the Downtown Push, usually known as just the Push. The Push was composed of several different elements. The most prominent component was, or were, the Libertarians – a university free-thought society consisting mainly of people who, like the aesthetes, failed Arts I on a career basis, but in this case as a form of political protest against the state. Endorsing Pareto's analysis of sexual guilt as a repressive social mechanism, the Libertarians freely helped themselves to each other's girlfriends. They had their own folk singer, Johnny Pitts, a hairy dwarf who every few minutes would flail his guitar, launch into a few bars of some barely comprehensible protest song about working conditions on an American railroad and fall sideways.

The next most prominent component was the aesthetes themselves, minus Keith Cameron but plus some specimens who were no longer to be seen around university, their nine years having finally run out. Without exception they were on the verge of writing, painting or composing something so marvellous that they did not want to run the risk of injuring it by rational analysis. As well as the Libertarians and the aesthetes there were small-time gamblers, traditional-jazz fans and the homosexual radio-repair men who had science fiction as a religion. A pick-up jazz band played loudly in the bar. The back room had tables and chairs. If you stuck your head through the door of the back room you came face to face with the Push. The noise, the smoke and the hetero-geneity of physiognomy were too much to take in. It looked like a cartoon on which Hogarth, Daumier and George Grosz had all worked together simultaneously, fighting for supremacy.

Nothing feels more like home than the place where the homeless gather. I was enchanted. Here was a paradise beyond the dreams of my mother or the Kogarah Presbyterian Church Fellowship. Here was Bohemia. I had friends here. Everyone in the Push borrowed money from everybody else. Happily I joined the circuit, forming a bad habit I was not to conquer for many years. Even in the rare evenings when Spencer or Huggins did not turn up, there was always Bottomley to talk to and borrow from, since this was the place where he made contact with his fellow gamblers. One of them was six feet six inches high and nicknamed Emu. Apart from his being permanently a thousand pounds in debt and in fear of his life, there was nothing remarkable about Emu except his mistress, but she was very remarkable indeed.

Her name was Lilith Talbot. About thirty years old, she was classically beautiful, with a discreetly ogival figure and a river of auburn hair. She was softly spoken and always elegantly dressed – two qualities which by themselves would have been enough to make her unique in those surroundings. What she saw in Emu was one of the great mysteries. Some said, crudely, that it was a matter of physiology: others, that it was an attraction between opposites. I adored her, first of all from afar, then from progressively closer to. She was openly delighted with my naive worship of all these people whose every secret she had known for years. She was probably also, I now realize, secretly delighted with my absurdly affected mimicry of Spencer. She accused me of being in love with him. I hotly denied the charge, even though it was partly true, and counter-attacked, greatly daring, by telling her that I was in love with her, which was wholly true. I tried to content myself with the prospect of a Platonic relationship. Not only was she entirely loyal to Emu, but Emu had friends who were almost as frightening as his enemies. The world of crime started just where the Push finished, and often the edges overlapped.

By this time my first poems were coming out in *honi soit*. They were, of course, the most abject pastiche, but my first appearance in print led me to an excess of posturing beside which Nerval walking his lobster would have been as inconspicuous as the Invisible Man. A symphony in corduroy velvet, smoking cigarettes the length of a blow-gun, I casually sprinted into Manning House, spread out a dozen copies of the paper, and read myself with ill-concealed approval. Even the patience of the Bellevue Hill mob was strained. They voted that I should no longer be heard on the subject of literature. Since the aesthetes grew equally tired of hearing their own opinions coming back at them, I was left with only Sally to berate during the day, and Lilith to harangue in the evening. They were bemused and long-suffering respectively. Heinrich Mann, writing about Nietzsche, remarks at one point that self-confidence often precedes achievement and is generally strained so long as it is untried. No self-confidence could have been more strained than mine. Underneath it, needless to say, lay gurgling indecision. The contradictions were piling up to such an altitude that it was getting hard to see over the top of them. On the one hand I was a petty-bourgeois student, on the other a libertarian bohemian. Sobbing into my beer in the Royal George, I predicted doom for myself in the forthcoming examinations. By day I nursed my hangover and meticulously took notes, wondering what the Push was up to. What was I missing out on?

When the exam results came out, I was deeply shocked to find that I had passed in both Anthropology and History, was listed in Order of Merit for English – i.e., midway between a pass and a credit – and had secured an outright credit in Psychology. Obviously the examiners had been moved to find their own lectures being returned to them in condensed form. Apart from Huggins, a star student in Architecture, none of the aesthetes had ever done as well in a lustrum as I had done in a year. I was neck and neck with the boys from Bellevue Hill. This made me feel guilty and alarmed. Which was I, a conformist or a nonconformist? I could feel my own personality coming apart like the original continental plates. Getting drunk was no solution, even though my mother was charmingly willing to accept the consequent behaviour as evidence of fatigue brought on by too much study. As I collapsed in the porch at midnight, having fallen over every garbage bin on the way down the street, I would explain to her that the Habsburgs had been too much for me. In a dressing gown with the hall light behind her, she looked down at her son, doubtless wondering what he was turning into. I was wondering the same thing.

Could there be such a thing as a virgin sophisticate? Had there ever been a man of the world who came home every night to his mother? Fate resolved this latter anomaly with brutal speed. My number came up and I found myself conscripted for National Service.

14. BASIC TRAINING

National Service was designed to turn boys into men and make the Yellow Peril think twice about moving south. It was universally known as Nasho – a typically Australian diminutive. Once you were in it, four years went by before you were out of it: there was a three-week camp every year, plus numerous parades. But the most brutal fact about Nasho was the initial seventy-seven-day period of basic training, most of which took place at Ingleburn. Each new intake of gormless youth was delivered into the hands of regular army instructors who knew everything about licking unpromising material into shape. When we stepped off the bus at Ingleburn, they were already screaming at us. Screaming sergeants and corporals appeared suddenly out of huts. I stood clutching my Globite suitcase and wondered what had gone wrong with my life. While I goggled at a screaming sergeant, I was abruptly blown sideways by a bellow originating from somewhere behind my right ear. Recovering, I turned to face Ronnie the One.

His real name was Warrant Officer First Class Ronald Mc-Donald, but he was known throughout the army as Ronnie the One. Responsible for battalion discipline, he had powers of life and death over all non-commissioned personnel and could even bring charges against officers up to the rank of captain. His appearance was almost inconceivably unpleasant. A pig born looking like him would have demanded plastic surgery. His brass gleamed like gold and his leather like mahogany, but the effect was undone by his khaki drills, which despite being ironed glass-smooth were perpet-ually soaked with sweat. Ronnie the One dripped sweat even on a cold day. It was not just because he was fat, although he had a

behind like an old sofa. It was because he was always screaming
so hard. At that moment he was screaming directly at me. 'GED
YAHAHCARDP!' Later on a translator told me that this meant 'Get
your hair cut' and could generally be taken as a friendly greeting,
especially if you could still see his eyes. When Ronnie was really
annoyed his face swelled up and turned purple like the rear end of
an amorous baboon.

For the next eleven weeks I was running flat out, but no matter
how fast my feet moved, my mind was moving even faster. It was
instantly plain to me that only cunning could ensure survival.
Among the university students in our intake, Wokka Clark was
undoubtedly the golden boy. Already amateur middleweight champion of NSW, he was gorgeous to behold. But he couldn't take the
bullshit. What happened to him was like a chapter out of *From
Here to Eternity*. They applauded him in the boxing ring at night
and screamed at him all day. That summer the noon temperature
was a hundred plus. Ronnie the One would take Wokka out on the
parade ground and drill him till he dropped. The reason Wokka
dropped before Ronnie did was simple. All Ronnie had on his head
was a cap. Wokka had on a steel helmet. The pack on his back was
full of bricks. After a few weeks of that, plus guard duty every night
that he wasn't boxing, even Wokka was obeying orders.

You couldn't fight them. Even the conscientious objectors
ended up looking after the regimental mascot – a bulldog called
Onslow who looked like Ronnie's handsome younger brother. It
was like one of Kenny Mears's games of marbles: nobody was
allowed not to play. I could appreciate the psychology of it. The
first task when training new recruits is to disabuse them of the
notion that life is fair. Otherwise they will stand rooted to the spot
when they first come up against people who are trying to kill them.
But my abstract understanding of what was going on impinged
only tangentially on the concrete problem of getting through the
day without landing myself in the kind of trouble that would make
the next day even more impossibly difficult than it was going to
be anyway.

Something about my general appearance annoyed Ronnie. There were a thousand trainees in the intake but I was among the select handful of those whose aspect he couldn't abide. I could be standing in a mess queue, Ronnie would be a dot in the distance, and suddenly his voice would arrive like incoming artillery. 'GEDDABIGGAHAD!' He meant that I should get a bigger hat. He didn't like the way it sat on top of my head. Perhaps he just didn't like my head, and wanted the whole thing covered up. The drill that I had learned in Boys' Brigade saved my life. When it came to square-bashing, it turned out that the years I had spent interpreting Captain Andrews's commands had given me a useful insight into what Ronnie was likely to mean by his shouts and screams. When Ronnie yelled 'ABARD HARGH!' I knew almost straight away that it must mean 'about turn'. Thus I was able to turn decisively with the many, instead of dithering with the few.

On the parade ground Peebles drew most of the lightning. So uncoordinated that he was to all intents and purposes a spastic, Peebles should not have been passed medically fit. But since he had been, the army was stuck with him. After a month of training, when Ronnie shouted, 'ABARD HARGH!' nine hundred and ninety-nine soldiers would smartly present their backs and Peebles would be writhing on the ground, strangled by the sling of his rifle. For Peebles the day of reckoning came when he obeyed an order to fix bayonets. This was one of Ronnie's most frightening orders. It had the verb at the end, as in German or Latin. In English the order would have sounded something like: 'Bayonets ... fix!' Bellowed by Ronnie, it came out as: 'BAHAYONED ... *FEE!*' The last word was delivered as a high-pitched, almost supersonic, scream. It was succeeded on this occasion by another scream, since Peebles' bayonet, instead of appearing at the end of his rifle, was to be seen protruding from the back of the soldier standing in front of him. After that, they used to mark Peebles present at company parade every morning but lose him behind a tree on the way to battalion parade, where he was marked absent.

My kit, not my drill, was what got me into trouble. For once in my life I had to make my own bed every morning, without fail, and lay out for inspection my neatly polished and folded belongings. Since the penalty for not doing this properly was to have the whole lot thrown on the floor and be obliged to start again, I gradually got better at it, but I never became brilliant. National Servicemen had to wax and polish their webbing instead of just powdering it with blanco. It was a long process which bored me, and the same fingers which had been so tacky at woodwork were still likely to gum up the job. The problem became acute when it was my platoon's turn to mount guard. Throughout the entire twenty-four hours it was on duty, the guard was inspected, supervised, harassed and haunted by Ronnie the One. The initial inspection of kit, dress and rifle lasted a full hour. Ronnie snorted at my brass, retched at my webbing and turned puce when he looked down the barrel of my rifle. 'THASSNODDAGHARDRIVAL!' he yelled. He meant that it was not a guard rifle. 'ISSFULLAPADAY-DAHS!' He meant that it was full of potatoes. I looked down the barrel. I had spent half a day pulling it through until it glowed like El Dorado's gullet. Now I saw that a single speck of grit had crept into it.

In the guardhouse we had to scrub the floors and tables, whitewash the walls and polish the undersides of the drawing pins on the notice board. When we went out on picket we could not afford to relax for a moment, since Ronnie could be somewhere in the vicinity preparing to do his famous Banzai charge. At two o'clock in the morning I was guarding the transport park. It was raining. Sitting down in the sentry box, I had the brim of my hat unbuttoned and was hanging from the collar of my groundsheet, praying for death. I had my rifle inside my groundsheet with me, so that I could fold my hands on its muzzle, lean my chin on the cushion formed by my hands under the cape and gently nod off while still looking reasonably alert. I had calculated that Ronnie would not come out in the rain. This proved to be a bad guess. I thought the sentry box had been struck by lightning, but it was merely Ronnie's face going off like a purple grenade about a foot in front of mine.

I came to attention as if electrocuted and tried to shoulder arms. Since the rifle was still inside my groundsheet, merely to attempt this manoeuvre was bound to yield Peebles-like results. Ronnie informed me, in a tirade which sounded and felt like an atomic attack, that he had never seen anything like it in his life.

The inevitable consequence was extra kitchen duty. I can safely say that I did more of this than anybody else in the battalion. While everybody else was out in the donga learning to disguise themselves as anthills and sneak up on the enemy, I was in the kitchen heading a crack team of cleaners composed of no-hopers like Peebles. The kitchen was as big as an aircraft hangar. All the utensils were on an enormous scale. The smallest dixies would be four feet long, two feet across and three feet deep. Lined with congealed custard and rhubarb, they took half an hour each to clean. The biggest dixie was the size of a Bessemer converter and mounted on gimbals. I was lowered into it on a rope. When I hit the bottom it rang like a temple gong. After the kitchen sergeant was satisfied that the dixie was shining like silver he pulled a crank and I was tipped out, smothered in mashed potato.

It must have been while I was inside the dixie that I missed out on the chance to volunteer for Infantry. That was how I found myself in the Assault Pioneers – the one specialist course that nobody sane wanted to be on, since it involved landmines, booby traps and detonators. In the long run the lethality of the subject proved to be a boon. National Service was winding to an end by that stage – ours was to be the last intake – and the government didn't want any mother's sons getting killed at the eleventh hour. So instead of burying mines for us to dig up, they buried rocks. While our backs were turned, they would bury a hundred rocks in a careful pattern. We would move through the area, probing the earth with our bayonets, and dig up two hundred. It wasn't as glamorous as being in, say, the mortar platoon, but I came to appreciate the lack of excitement, especially after we were all marched out to the range and given a demonstration of what the mortar specialists had learned.

The mortars in question were the full three inches across the barrel – not the two-inch pipes that had little more than nuisance value, but really effective weapons which could throw a bomb over a mountain and kill everything within a wide radius at the point of impact. A thousand of us, including the colonel and all his officers, sat around the rim of a natural amphitheatre while the mortar teams fired their weapons. All looked downwards at the mortars with fascination, except for Ronnie the One, who was down with the mortars looking upwards, tirelessly searching for anyone with too small a hat. Team after team loaded and fired. The bomb was dropped into the mortar and immediately departed towards the stratosphere, where it could be heard – and even, momentarily, seen – before it dived towards its target, which was a large cross on a nearby hill. You saw the blast, then you heard the sound. It was a bit like watching Ronnie having a heart attack on the horizon.

Every team did its job perfectly until the last. The last team was Wokka Clark and Peebles. They had to do *something* with Peebles. If they had put him in the Pioneers he probably would have bitten the detonator instead of the fuse. It went without saying that he could not be allowed to drive a truck or fire a Vickers machine gun, especially after the way he had distinguished himself on the day everyone in the battalion had had to throw a grenade. (One at a time we entered the throwing pit. The sergeant handed you a grenade, from which you removed the pin. You then threw the grenade. When he handed Peebles a grenade, Peebles removed the pin and handed the grenade back to him.) The safest thing to do with Peebles was team him up with Wokka, who was so strong that he could throw the base plate of a three-inch mortar twenty yards. All Peebles had to do was wait until Wokka had done the calibrations and then drop in the bomb. He must have done it successfully scores of times in practice. He did it quite smoothly this time too, except that the bomb went in upside down.

If you were to rig a vacuum cleaner to blow instead of suck and then point it at a pile of dust, you would get some idea of what those thousand supposedly disciplined men did a split second after they noticed the bomb going into the mortar with its fins sticking up instead of down. They just melted away. Some tried to dig themselves into the earth. Some started climbing trees. But most of us ran. I was running flat out when an officer went past me at head height, flapping his arms like a swan. Ronnie stopped the panic by shouting 'HARD!', meaning 'halt'. The noise could have been the bomb going off, but since it was unaccompanied by shrapnel it seemed safe to pay attention. Everyone turned and looked down. Ronnie picked up the whole mortar, base plate included, shook out the bomb and handed it to Peebles. Silence. Wokka still had his hands over his eyes. Peebles dropped the bomb in the right way up. The mortar coughed. There was a crackle in the sky and a blast on the hill. Then we all marched thoughtfully back to camp.

By now I had made a career out of being a private. Having made the mistake of supplying all the right answers in the intelligence test (since it was exactly the same test that I had been studying in Psychology I, this was no great feat), I was at first put under some pressure to become an officer, or failing that an NCO. But it soon became clear to all concerned that I was a born private. I had revived my joker persona as a means of ingratiating myself with my fellow conscripts. I had no wish to lose their approval by being raised above them. Nor was I morally equipped to accept responsibility for others. But I did manage to get better at being the lowest form of life in the army. I was a digger. I learned the tricks of looking neat without expending too much energy. And although it would have been heresy to say so, I actually enjoyed weapons training. I had the eyes to be good at firing the .303 rifle, but not the hands. Yet I relished being instructed on it. And the Bren was such a perfect machine that there was avid competition to specialize. I never got to the stage of wanting to sleep with one, but must admit that there were times when, as I eyed the Bren's sleek lines, I discovered in myself a strong urge to fiddle with its gas-escape regulator.

The weapons sergeants were all regular soldiers with combat experience, usually in Korea. There was virtue, it seemed to me, in

listening when they talked. They were wise in their craft. Every
few intakes one of them got shot by a National Serviceman. None
of them wanted to be the one. After surviving a long encounter
with half a million glory-hungry Chinese it makes no sense to be
finished off by some adolescent pointing his rifle at you and saying,
'Sergeant, it's stuck.' They were particularly careful when it came
to instructing us on the Owen machine carbine. This was the same
gun I had once carted around Jannali. The Owen cocked itself if
you dropped it and shot you when you picked it up. It disgorged
fat, 9mm slugs at a very high rate of fire and the barrel clawed up
to the right during the burst. If due precautions were not taken,
the man on the left of the line would mow down everyone else,
including the instructor. The sergeants were very cautious about
whom they put on the left, and always stood well to the left
themselves. Some of them stood so far to the left they were out of
sight. Without exception they refused to let Peebles fire the thing
at all. They parked him behind his usual tree on the way to the
range and faked his score.

I also enjoyed drill. Einstein once said that any man who liked
marching had been given his brain for nothing: just the spinal
column would have done. But I wasn't Einstein. Since most of
one's time in the army is wasted anyway, I preferred to waste it by
moving about in a precise manner. It was better than blueing my
pay packet at a pontoon game in the lavatories. As fit as I would
ever be in my life, I could fling a Lee-Enfield .303 rifle around like
a baton. When I was ordered to volunteer as right front marker for
the exhibition drill squad, I sensibly said yes. Saying no would have
immediately entailed being lowered into the big dixie, so it was
scarcely a courageous decision.

The drill squad was one of the star items on the big day.
Visiting brass and proud parents lined the parade ground. Dressed
in white singlets, khaki drill trousers, gaiters and boots, ninety-nine
strapping examples of bronzed young Australian manhood all took
their time from me. We looked like an erotic dream by Leni
Riefenstahl. Ronnie gave the orders in his usual mixture of Urdu

and epilepsy, but by now I could read his mind. Miraculously dry-handed in the heat, I put the .303 through its paces. It was all a matter of not worrying. Just let the body remember. It wasn't until the routine was over and we were marching off to a storm of applause that the thought occurred to me: they had done it. They had got what they wanted out of me. But on the other hand I had got what I wanted out of them. I had acquired my first real measure of self-sufficiency, which is something other, and quieter, than mere self-assertion, and probably the opposite of being self-absorbed.

That night the whole drill squad was given leave. Blazing with brass and polished green webbing, I got off the train in Sydney after sunset and headed straight for the Royal George, marching an inch above the pavement in my mirror-finish boots. There was a roar of scorn as I entered the back room. Cries of 'Fascist!' rose from all sides. But for once I was sure of myself. Nobody looking as unappealing as the Libertarians was in a position to sneer at the starched perfection of my KDs. Johnny Pitts flailed his guitar, launched into a few bars of some barely comprehensible protest song about American militarism and fell sideways. Grogan, saluting wildly, jumped up and down on a table. Once again he was clad in nothing but G-string Speedo and thongs. Spencer was pretending to be dazzled by my beauty. Everyone was in character. It all passed me by, because I had noticed that Emu was not present. Lilith Talbot was unaccompanied.

I suppose it was just my lucky night. Emu, it transpired, was somewhere in the Blue Mountains, hiding from some people who had threatened to dip him by the heels in Hen and Chicken Bay, a part of the harbour much favoured by grey nurse sharks. From the goodness of her simple heart, Lilith told me straight away that it would be a pity if we did not take advantage of this opportunity to complete my basic training. But it could happen only once, and there must never be a word to anyone, or my death would follow shortly upon hers. Did I understand that? Transfixed by the shape of her mouth, I nodded dumbly. We walked out of the room together – a sound tactic, since it looked too intimate to be anything but innocent. And if I couldn't believe my luck, all those other helplessly doting males would be doing their best not to believe my luck either.

On the ferry to Kirribilli we sat on a bench in the prow. It was a warm night in late summer. The breeze would have ruffled Lilith's hair if her hair had been less heavy. A junkyard of light, Luna Park spilled ladders of pastel across the water, the Big Dipper roaring like a wounded dragon. Under the deck of the Harbour Bridge, the ultraviolet beacon that guides the big ships through the dark sent out its cobwebs of lapis lazuli above our heads. I made Lilith look up at it. She let me kiss her. I didn't know it was allowed. I kept expecting a squad of MPs to appear and place me under arrest.

But there was just us. Walking up the hill was like being shown into Olympus by a resident. Everything she had on must have weighed about two ounces all told. A pale-blue cotton dress and a pair of gracile high-heeled white sandals were all that I could see. I didn't know what to do with my hands, but somehow everything was all right. It went on being all right when we got to her place. Really the house belonged to Emu. It was his one tangible asset. Lilith had a room in it of her own, although even here there were signs of Emu's pre-eminence. A crate of empty beer bottles against the wall could belong only to him. The same applied to the 16lb shot on top of the cupboard. In a previous incarnation Emu had been GPS shot-put champion.

Lilith opened the curtains towards where the sun would be when it came up. It seemed that nothing but darkness was there now. But when she turned out the light, there was still enough illumination to reach her. She took her dress off over her head and stood there while my eyes began the long task of getting used to seeing what before they had only imagined. For Lilith, her own beauty was a sufficient reason to exist. I would like to be able to say that we celebrated her loveliness together. In fact I hardly knew what I was doing. She was more tolerant than I was capable of realizing. I had no idea of delay, and would not have been able to do much about it even if I had. It was all too exciting. What an older and wiser man would have made last for hours was all over in seconds. I gave a spasmodic lurch and kicked the cupboard. The shot rolled off the top of it and fell into the crate of beer bottles. I was too pleased with myself to care. Lilith Talbot is among my fondest memories. And you can stop thinking that she's a figment of my imagination. Of course she is.

15. VERY WELL: ALONE

The last week of basic training was spent on bivouac at Singleton. The whole battalion camped out in the donga. Our company was instructed to storm and fortify the top of a mountain. My Pioneer platoon was ordered to dig a command post out of the virgin rock. Since there was no dynamite, we had to do it with picks and shovels. After six days the command post was three inches deep. If the battalion had been commanded by leprechauns it would have been an ideal headquarters. I didn't care. I could still taste Lilith. Periodically there was a tremendous hullabaloo as a pair of RAAF Sabre jets went past below us. They were pretending to strafe the infantry who were fitfully shooting blanks at each other down in the valley.

Around the campfire at night I was the expert on sex. I was still a long way away from learning that the main difference between an adult and an adolescent is the ability to keep secrets. I betrayed Lilith dreadfully, even to the extent of telling them her real name. But everybody else was too drunk to notice. The mortar platoon kept us in fresh meat. Accidentally on purpose they blew a cow to smithereens. One moment it was grazing contentedly and the next it was spread all over the landscape. Every platoon got a smithereen each. We roasted it over the fire and washed it down with wine bought in bulk from a vineyard in the next valley. The wine was so raw that it left your tongue looking like a crocodile-skin handbag.

A fat soldier called Malouf had stolen my position as chief joker. He sang a hundred choruses of 'Old King Cole' and fainted into the fire. But in my new role of sex expert I had enough confidence to serve out my time. It was steep up that mountain.

We slept under groundsheets rigged as pup tents. It was advisable to pitch your tent in close contact with the trunk of a stout tree, otherwise you could end up as part of an avalanche. With my feet sticking out of one end of the tent and my head out of the other I looked straight up at the stars. There were stars between the stars. The mountain air was unmixed, as in Dante's Paradise: you could see to the edge of the universe. The Southern Cross was so brilliant that it dripped. You could have picked it out of the sky and hung it around a young nun's neck. I had never felt more alive. From miles away below came the occasional snapping of dry sticks and what sounded like the muffled howl of a wombat being raped. It was Ronnie, Banzai-charging the sentries.

Buoyant with well-being, I returned to civilian life. Between the top of Margaret Street and our front gate my mother came to meet me. I knew that look, so my mental defence mechanisms were already going into action when she told me that Gary Meldrum had been killed the day before racing his motorbike at Mount Druitt. I learned the details later on. He had been leading a pack of AJS 7Rs when his telescopic front fork collapsed on a bend. The bike went up in the air with its throttle stuck open and when it came back down again he was lying underneath it. The chain cut his throat and he died instantly.

I walked my mother inside and made her a cup of tea. I didn't feel anything at all except a sense that I was falling upwards from the past. It was all going away from me. I could feel a vacuum plucking at the back of my shirt. After the funeral service at Kogarah Presbyterian Church I cried noisily in the street but it was the kind of reflex that would have pleased the Sydney University Psychology Department, since it was unconnected with anything going on in my head. I began to suspect that I might have nothing in there except scar tissue, or else a couple of loose wires that should have been touching each other but weren't.

Being a mother's boy is a condition that can be fully cured only by saying goodbye to mother. Nevertheless I did not entirely revert. I was soon having my bed made for me again, but I managed to keep something of my new-found independence. Justifying callousness as necessary for survival, I did pretty much what I pleased. The rest of my university course was a steadily accelerating story of possibilities explored and studies neglected. Lilith and I were just friends again, alas. On the other hand she had spoiled me for little girls who, in the charming jargon of that time, did not come across. So I left Sally Vaughan in tears, went in search of something less complicated, and had my wishes granted often enough to ensure that the moment of real involvement in somebody else's life went on being put off into the indeterminate future, whose outline looked as hazy as ever. All that I could be sure of was that some form of writing would play a part in it.

I went on to become literary editor of *honi soit*, with a page of my own to look after every week. Almost invariably I filled it with my own productions. Some of them were so pretentious that even today I can't recall their tone without emitting an involuntary yell of anguish. But a certain fluency accrued from the sheer exercise, and inevitably a certain notoriety accrued along with it. There was a shimmering before my eyes. Narcissus was beginning the long process of getting his reflection in focus.

The need to be approved of aided my progress, if progress it was. I never stopped admiring the talent of Spencer and Keith Cameron, but gradually at first, and then quicker all the time, my own activities took a different course. The desire to amuse overcame the desire to shock. By my second year I was already writing a good proportion of the Revue, and by my third year I was writing almost half of it. Against my will but according to my instincts, I recognized that when I mimicked Spencer's mannerisms I made no connection with the audience, and that when what I wrote was my own idea, the audience laughed. I tried to hold them in contempt for that, but could not quite succeed. So I tried to hold myself in contempt instead, but could not quite succeed at that either. It was already occurring to me that in these matters practice might be wiser than theory.

If only everything had been clearer. If I had read Sartre at that stage I might have learned that the obligation to create one's life from day to day was an inescapable responsibility. Luckily I read Camus instead. Here was my first mature literary enthusiasm: instead of merely having my prejudices confirmed, I was disabused of them. Camus offered consolation by telling you that yours was not the only personality which felt as if it was lying around in pieces – every life felt like that from the inside. More importantly, he offered a moral vision that went beyond the self. 'Tyrants conduct monologues above a million solitudes.' I looked at a sentence like that until my eyes grew tired. It wasn't poetry. So why was it so poetic? How did he do it? And where could I buy a coat like his? I tilted my head to the same angle, practised lighting a Disque Bleu so that the flame atmospherically lit the lower half of my face and planned to die in a car crash.

The immature enthusiasms continued along with the mature ones. I went crazy for Ezra Pound. I unhesitatingly incorporated the manic self-confidence of his critical manner into my own prose. Since my ignorance far outstripped even his, I was lucky not to fall further under his spell. Once again instinct was wiser than thought. Even when I was drunk with awe at the sheer incomprehensibility of the *Cantos*, I was simultaneously delighting in the clear, strong, sane talent of MacNeice. When I came to read Yeats I soon saw what real grandeur was, and realized that Pound's grandiloquence was not it.

The Great Gatsby helped teach me what a real prose style was like. I read it over and over. Even at that early stage I could see that if it came to a choice between Hemingway and Fitzgerald, I would take Fitzgerald – not just because his cadences were more seductive, but because he was less sentimental. I never let it come to the choice, preferring to admire them both. I went mad on the Americans generally. E. E. Cummings made me drunk. Mencken's sceptical high spirits seemed to me the very tones of ebullient sanity. It went without saying that there was no question of being interested in Australian culture as such. Nobody had given it a thought in the last twenty years.

Having finished reading Keith Cameron's library, I started
reading the university library, which was named after someone
called Fisher. In those days Fisher Library was housed in a building
which looked like the little brother of Milan Cathedral and formed
part of the Quad. But even when I was wearing a groove up and
down the library stairs I was always careful not to read anything
on the course. If the syllabus said Beaumont and Fletcher, I read
Mencken and Nathan. If it said Webster and Ford, I read Auden
and Isherwood. Life would have been so much simpler had I done
what I was asked that today I never stop wondering why I didn't.
Two or three of the English lecturers were of world class. I
assiduously contrived never to learn anything about Old English.
I faked my way through that part of the course by memorizing the
cribs. It was only my ability to conjure a fluent essay out of thin
air that got me admitted to the third year of the honours school.
That, and the incidental benefit of reading Shakespeare morning,
noon and night. There, for once, I got the horse before the cart.

Psychology I gave up at the end of the second year, just before
it gave up me. When it came to statistical analysis, I was helpless.
A deep spiritual aversion to the whole subject might also have had
something to do with it. Not even Freud appealed. I could see the
poetic fecundity of his imagination, but as an actor in a real-life
Oedipus play I felt free to question his teleological sophistry.
Undoubtedly, my father having mysteriously been killed, I had
inherited exclusive rights to my mother's favours. But to suggest
that either of the two survivors had in any way desired such an
outcome was patently ludicrous. I got through the psychology
examinations on a 'post' – i.e., a viva voce after having written
a borderline paper. I would not have been granted even the 'post'
if it had not been for my clinical case study. During the course of
the year we had to assemble an elaborate case study of some real
person. My clinical study was little Toni Turrell, sexy Shirley's
sister. Five minutes into the Wechsler–Bellevue intelligence test I
realized that little Toni was a hopeless moron who would yield up
the same personality profile as a block of wood. So I excused her

from any further tests and cooked up the whole thing. It was, if I may say so, a brilliantly convincing job. 'Toni: A Case Study' was my first attempt at a full-length fictional work. (This book is the second.)

Anthropology also moved to a natural demise at the end of the second year. It was only a two-year subject anyway. Having absorbed the contents of *Frigging Around in Fiji* and regurgitated them at the appropriate moment, I was rewarded with the minimum pass. Education I, which I sat in my second year, I failed outright. I can see now that this result was an instinctively correct estimate of the subject's importance, but at the time it fitted in with a familiar pattern. Since my mind, or at any rate my heart, was already on some other path, I was not as worried as I might have been about the growing evidence that my attention was wandering from my work. But for my mother the whole meandering dereliction was all too disturbingly recognizable, especially now that I was more often arriving home early the next morning instead of late that night, and then late the next night instead of in the early morning.

Between my second and third years I tried to recoup my position in the parental eye by getting a job in the long vacation. I was accepted as a trainee bus conductor. The buses were green Leyland diesels operating out of Tempe depot. The easy routes went overland to places like Bexley and Drummoyne. The difficult routes went through the city. I found the job fiercely demanding even on a short route with a total of about two dozen passengers. I pulled the wrong tickets, forgot the change and wrote up my log at the end of each trip in a way that drew hollow laughter from the inspectors. The inspectors were called Kellies, after Ned Kelly, and were likely to swoop at any time. A conductor with twenty years' service could be dismissed if a Kelly caught him accepting money without pulling a ticket. If a hurrying passenger pressed the fare into your hand as he leapt out of the back door, it was wise to tear a ticket and throw it out after him. There might be a plainclothes Kelly following in an unmarked car.

Days of fatigue and panic taught me all over again that I am very bad at what I am not good at. We worked a split shift with four hours off in the middle of the day. Effectively this meant that we were on the job twelve hours a day, since there was nothing else to do with the four hours off except hang around the depot. I got so tired I used to sleep the whole four hours on a bench in the billiard room. Once I conked out with a lighted Rothmans in my hand. I dreamed of a bushfire burning down Jannali school with Miss Turnbull still inside it. I woke to face a cloud of smoke. The whole front of my shirt had burned away. The billiard room was full of conductors and drivers who had been placing bets on when I would wake up. The white nylon singlet I had been wearing under the shirt was scorched the colour of strong tea.

I lasted about three weeks all told, which meant that I hardly got past probation. The routes through town were more than the mind could stand even in the off-peak hours. In peak hours the scene was Dantesque. All the buses from our depot and every other depot would be crawling nose to tail through town while the entire working population of Sydney fought to get aboard. It was hot that summer: 100°F every day. Inside the bus it was 30° hotter still. Hammering up Pitt Street in the solid traffic at about ten miles an hour, the bus was like the Black Hole of Calcutta on wheels. It was so jammed inside that my feet weren't touching the floor. I couldn't blink the sweat out of my eyes. There was no hope of collecting any fares. At each stop it was all I could do to reach the bell-push that signalled the driver to close the automatic doors and get going. I had no way of telling whether anybody had managed to get off or on. My one object was to get that bus up Pitt Street. Passengers fainted and just hung there – there was nowhere for them to fall. The air tasted as if it had just been squirted out of the safety valve of a pressure cooker full of cabbage. In those circumstances I was scarcely to blame. I didn't even know where we were, but I guessed we were at the stop just before Market Street. I pressed the bell, the doors puffed closed, and the bus surged forward. There were shouts and yells from down the back, but I thought they were the angry cries of passengers who had not got on. Too slowly I realized that they were emanating from within the bus. The back set of automatic doors had closed around an old lady's neck as she was getting on. Her head, wearing a black veiled hat decorated with wax fruit, was inside the bus. The rest of her, carrying a shopping bag with each hand, was outside. I knew none of this at the time. When I at last cottoned on to the fact that something untoward was happening and signalled the driver to stop, he crashed to a halt and opened the automatic doors, whereupon the woman dropped to the road. She was very nice about it. Perhaps the experience had temporarily dislocated her mind. Anyway, she apologized to me for causing so much trouble. Unfortunately the car just behind turned out to be full of Kellies. Since it would have made headlines if a university student had been thrown off the buses for half-guillotining a woman of advanced years, I was given the opportunity to leave quietly. Once again this failed to coincide with my own plans only in the sense that I had already resigned. In fact I had made my decision at about the same time as the old lady hit the ground.

16. FIDGETY FEET

Nor, in my last year, did I prove to be any better as a student than I had been as a bus conductor. I no longer saw fit to attend any lectures at all. But my extracurricular activities flourished, following the principle that I could be infinitely energetic in those areas where it didn't matter. The Revue that year had my name in the programme thirty-two times. As well as writing most of the sketches, I was assistant producer to a man called Waldo Laidlaw, an advertising executive who was prominent in fringe theatre. Spencer and Keith Cameron despised Waldo's stylishness but I couldn't help being fascinated. He ranked as the local Diaghilev. Under his aegis, the Revue's costumes and decor took on an unmistakably self-confident look – a fact which could be easily detected by the naked eye, since Waldo was in favour of turning the lights right up. Most of the numbers I wrote were so embarrassing that I can't recall them even when I try, but others had the sort of half-success with the audience that fans the desire to go further.

By now I was writing a good half of *honi soit* every week. The letters column was full of protests about things I had written. The letters of protest were nearly all written by me. A certain kind of cheap fame accumulated, in which I pretended not to wallow. More significantly, the *Sydney Morning Herald* asked me to review books. The editor was Angus Maude, who at the time was serving out the bleak years after Suez, before returning to Britain and resuming his climb to influence. I owe Angus Maude a great deal. The bread of exile must have been bitter enough without having my cocksure ignorance to cope with on top of it. The first reviews

I wrote for him were too pig-headed to be publishable. His simplest course would have been to forget the whole idea. But by a series of gentle hints he induced me to write within the scope of what I knew, so that I could turn out a piece which, while it did not fail to be dull, was at least seldom outright foolish.

Tom Fitzgerald, editor of a new literary-cum-political weekly called the *Nation*, was the next to pick me up. He had already hired Huggins. Fitzgerald treated me with great patience. A man of real learning, he also had the gusto to value keenness even when it was uninformed. In Vadim's, the King's Cross coffee bar where he held court, I would join the table late at night and pipe fatuous comments from my position below the salt. The other, more venerable literary men present stared deep into their glasses of Coonawarra claret or hurriedly reminisced, but Tom went on being tolerant even after the catastrophic week when I succeeded in reviewing the same book both for his magazine and the *Herald*. The Gaggia espresso machine hissed and gurgled. The six-foot blonde waitress swayed and swooped. Huggins blew in with a sheaf of new drawings. This was the life. The Royal George started seeming less attractive, especially when you considered that Emu was likely to be sitting in it. He had a new way of staring at me that made me feel cold and sticky, like a very old ice-cube.

Getting my name in the papers helped ease the transition from the last year of university to the first year of real life. My honours degree in English was scarcely of the highest grade, but there was no need to tell my mother that the result was really less impressive than it looked, and besides, in the same week that the results came out the *Herald* offered me a job. I was only to be assistant to the editor of the magazine page of the Saturday edition, but it felt unsettlingly like success. As if to redeem myself for betraying their uncompromising standards, I spent many evenings that summer with Spencer and Grogan, bucketing across the Harbour Bridge in Grogan's wreck of a Chevrolet to crash parties on the North Shore. Unfortunately I found it less easy than they did to hate what was to be found there. The young men of the North Shore might exceed even the Bellevue Hill mob in their partiality for cravats and suede shoes, but some of the girls were uncomfortably appealing. I resented their gentle manners but not from superiority. What unsettled me about the people of the North Shore was the way they all knew each other. I was, am and will continue to be until the grave, incurably envious of all families.

But I was flattered to find that my name was already known. While Grogan was being thrown out and Spencer was being aloof in a canvas chair beside the swimming pool, I would be queuing at the wine cask or holding forth near the barbecue. It seemed to me that the girls hung on my words. It seemed that they were positively leaning sideways to drink them in. Then the lawn would swing up and hit me. After just such an exploit a girl called Françoise drove me back to town. She was a diplomat's daughter. Infuriatingly she could read Latin, French and German, looked marvellously pretty and would not let me sleep with her. She offered something called Friendship instead, which I grudgingly accepted. After vomiting into the glove compartment of her Renault Dauphine, I felt I owed her the time of day.

My year at the *Herald* can be briefly recounted. The editor of the Saturday magazine page was a veteran journalist called Leicester Cotton. He was a sweet man whose days of adventure were long behind. We shared a partitioned-off cubicle just big enough to hold two desks. While he got on with choosing the serials and book excerpts which would fill the main part of the page, it was my task to rewrite those unsolicited contributions which might just make a piece. All I had to do was change everything in them and they would be fine. Apart from the invaluable parsing lessons at school, these months doing rewrites were probably the best practical training I ever received. Characteristically I failed to realize it at first. But gradually the sheer weight of negative evidence began to convince me that writing is essentially a matter of saying things in the right order. It certainly has little to do with the creative urge per se. Invariably the most prolific contributors were the ones who could not write a sentence without saying the opposite of what they meant. One man, resident in Woy Woy, sent us a new novel every month. Each novel took the form of twenty thick exercise books held together in a bundle. Each exercise book was full to the brim with neat handwriting. The man must have written more compulsively than Enid Blyton, who at least stopped for the occasional meal. Unlike Enid Blyton, however, he could not write even a single phrase that made any sense at all.

But the contributors most to be dreaded were the ones who came to call. Down-at-heel, over-the-hill journalists would waste hours of Leicester's time discussing their plans to interview Ava Gardner. Any of them would have stood a better chance with Mary, Queen of Scots. Even the most sprightly of them was too far gone to mind spoiling the effect of his wheeler-dealer dialogue by producing in mid-spiel a defeated sandwich from the pocket of his grimy tan gabardine overcoat. One character used to drop in personally in order to press for the return of articles which he had never sent. Another was in charge of a pile of old newspapers so heavy that he had to drag it. He was like a dung beetle out of Karel Čapek. Our office was a transit camp for dingbats. Every form of madness used to come through that door. It was my first, cruel exposure to the awkward fact that the arts attract the insane. They arrived in relays from daylight to dusk. For all the contact they had with reality, they might as well have been wearing flippers, rotating bow ties and sombreros with model trains running around the brim.

No wonder Leicester was relieved when his old journalist friend Herb Grady dropped in. Herb Grady bored me stiff with his endless talk of old times but at least he looked normal. He used to come in every morning about an hour before lunch, which he took in the Botanical Gardens. He was retired by then, so I assumed that the small leather case he always carried contained sandwiches and a Thermos of tea. I could imagine the tea growing cold even with its silver shell as Herb reminisced interminably on. Leicester didn't seem to mind, however. Then one day, as Herb was getting up to leave, the hasp on the leather case snapped open and the sole contents fell clattering to the floor. It was a single ice-skate.

Probably because I found the work easy to cope with, I felt as if I were marking time. Like most people who feel that, I hung around my old haunts. That year I directed the Union Revue. Despite my tenaciously lingering pretensions, those items emanating from my pen attained a hitherto unheard-of perspicuity. I also discovered within myself a knack of delegating authority – which essentially means recognizing your own limitations and deputing others to do well what you yourself would only muck up. The show was called *A Rat up a Pump*. It came in on budget and showed a profit. The audience, if it did not go home happy, at least stayed to the end. At the back of the hall I preened unobtrusively, praying that one of the actors would get sick so that I could go on instead. The one who did was the cast midget. Since all the sketches he was in depended for their point on his diminutive stature (he was about eighteen inches high in his elevator shoes) trying to get his laughs was something of a challenge.

It was the only challenge of that year. Even Françoise finally yielded, although wisely she never ceased to be suspicious. I rather liked the idea of being thought of as a shit – a common conceit among those who don't realize just how shitty they really are. In retrospect I wonder that she put up with me for a single day. The boredom must have been tremendous, since on top of all my other affectations I was going through an acute Salinger phase, starting off as Holden Caulfield and ending up as Seymour Glass. She managed not to burst out laughing when I casually declared my intention of learning Sanskrit. She no doubt guessed that some other influence would drive that remote possibility even further into the distance, although it could have given her no pleasure to discover that my next persona, when it arrived, had been borrowed from Albert Finney in *Saturday Night and Sunday Morning*. Lurching from the cinema with my hands crammed into my pockets to guard them from the northern cold, I waited for my breath to form a cloud before my face. Since it was ninety in the shade, this was not on the cards, but the Flash of Lightning was a long time hanging up his cape.

Things were getting a bit too easy. On the other hand, there was growing evidence that they were also getting a bit meaningless. There was nothing I knew worth knowing. Françoise was a model of tact, but occasionally she would unintentionally reveal that she had actually read, in the original language, some of the authors upon whose lack of talent I pronounced so glibly. Unable to fool her, I could not hope to go on fooling myself. Slowly it began occurring to me that the ability to get things done was a combination of two elements, the desire to do them and the capacity to take pains. The mind had to be both open and single. I had always shared the general opinion that Dave Dalziel, one of my student contemporaries, was faintly ludicrous, since he was so fanatical about films that he kept notebooks in which every film he saw was graded according to twenty different criteria. Then he suddenly started making a film using all his friends as actors. It took a year to complete. I had turned down his invitation to write the script. Someone else did it instead. When I saw the film I was envious. It was no more awful than my own work. More importantly, it was *there*. Abruptly I realized that Dave Dalziel was there too. What he had done once he would do again. It also occurred to me that those who had laughed at him loudest were the least likely ever to do anything themselves. Not that Dave kept his public short of reasons to shake their heads over him. One weekend about a dozen car-loads full of aesthetes and theatricals drove south to hold a bush picnic near Thirroul. I was braced in the back of Grogan's Chevrolet along with Bottomley and Wanda. Spencer was in the front seat, navigating. Navigation consisted of tailing the car in front – never easy with Grogan driving, since he was unable to go slower than flat out. Despite looking as if it had been gutted by a hollow charge, the Chevrolet could do a true eighty. Dave's Jaguar Mk IV went past us as if we were standing still. Dave was standing back to front on the driving seat with his head, shoulders and torso

all protruding through the sunshine roof. He was waving a bottle
of wine at us. That night around the campfire I learned that his
long-legged girlfriend had had one foot on the accelerator, one
hand on the wheel and the other hand inside Dave's trousers.
Something else he told me that night was that he believed his
future lay in England. He seemed to know exactly where he was
going. Thoughtfully I helped to put the fire out by hurling on it
and crawled into a sleeping bag with Wanda. Kissing her was like
cleaning an ashtray with your tongue.

Huggins came back from a trip to Europe. In London he had
actually met T. S. Eliot. Within a month he was on his way to
New York, riding in one of the Boeing 707 jet airliners which had
by now succeeded the old Stratocruisers, Super Constellations and
Douglas DC-7s in the eternal task of shaking our house to its
foundations. In Huggins I could clearly see the reality of talent, as
opposed to the rhetoric of pretension. What he said he would do,
he would do. What he did was in demand. He was on his way.

Something told me it was time to move. I still don't know what
it was. Is it restlessness that tells us we are not at rest? Such
questions invite tautologies for answers. Actually we all got the
same idea at once. It was just that I was among the first of that
particular generation to make the break. Suddenly everyone was
heading towards England. We were like those pelagic birds whose
migratory itinerary is pricked out in their minds as an overlay on
the celestial map, so that when you release them inside a planet-
arium they fly in the wrong direction, but still according to their
stars. I drew my severance pay from the *Herald* and bought a £97
one-way passage on a ship leaving at the very end of the year.
As I should have expected, my mother, when I gaily informed her
of my plans, reacted as Dido might have done if Aeneas had sent
a barber-shop quartet to tell her that he had decided to leave
Carthage. She was simultaneously distraught and insulted. But my
callousness won out. Plainly I would get my way even in this. How
could I be sure of that, unless I had been spoilt? So it was all her
fault, really.

In that summer of 1961 I was seldom home to be made impatient by what I considered her unreasoning grief. During the week I slept on sundry floors, infested the coffee bars and swam with Françoise at Bronte and Bondi. At the weekends I went north with the Bellevue Hill mob to Frank Chine's old house at Avalon. Gilbert Bolt's cousin used the place as a weekender. Consisting mainly of verandas, it could sleep half a dozen people comfortably and a dozen uncomfortably. We swam all day at Palm Beach, got drunk at night and were woken in the morning by the whip birds and the kookaburras. The girls wore sandals, white shorts, T-shirts and a dab of zinc cream on their noses. Walking back from the shops with meat for the barbecue, they were apparitions in the heat haze, dreams within a dream. I never drew a sober breath. The mosquitoes who found a way inside my net at night got too drunk to find their way out again. On Christmas Eve I woke at ten in the morning with a shattering hangover to find that my bare feet, which had been tilted skyward over the rail of the veranda, were burned shocking pink on the soles.

The last days ticked away. I packed in an hour, carefully ignoring all advice about warm clothes. The ship sailed on New Year's Eve of 1961. She was called the *Bretagne* – an ex-French 29,000-ton liner now flying Greek colours. The point of departure was the new international terminal at Circular Quay. After nightfall the farewell party swarmed all over the deck. All around the quay echoed the confused noises of music, laughter, sobbing and regurgitation. The water around the ship was lit up so brightly it was as if there were lights below the surface. It was a cloudy pastel green, like colloidal jade. The deck was jammed. Hundreds of people were leaving and thousands had come to see them off. Johnny Pitts should have been going. His intention had been to go to Cuba and 'fight for anarchy'. Unfortunately in the place where his passport application required him to state his profession he had put 'Anarchist'. So he was not allowed to leave.

But the whole Push had turned up anyway. If the Push didn't crash it, it wasn't a party. They brought the Royal George jazz band

with them. All the Bellevue Hill mob were there. One of the two
rugby players sharing my cabin was of their number. Some of the
Bellevue Hill mob were there to say goodbye to me as well. Spencer
and Keith Cameron, Wanda and Bottomley turned up specifically
to wish me luck. My mother was there. Françoise was there too,
not saying very much. Probably she was still pondering my valedic-
tory oration of the day before. On Bondi beach, with her neat body
sheltering me from the sandy prickle of the Southerly Buster, I had
intrepidly told her that I would be gone five years, and advised her
to forget me. I suppose I expected to be admired for this heroic
stance. As with all instinctive role-players, my first expectation was
that other people would recognize the scene and play their part
accordingly. Nor, to be fair to myself, could I see why anybody
should miss me. Excessive conceit and deficient self-esteem are
often aspects of each other.

The last craneloads of shish kebab and moussaka came swinging
aboard. The party was reaching its frenzied height. The jazz band
shouted 'Black Bottom Stomp'. I stood crammed into a bunch with
my mother, Françoise, the ever-polite Keith Cameron and half a
dozen other well-wishers. Every other passenger was surrounded
by a similar tight circle. Suddenly a narrow path of silence opened
towards us through the crowd. She always had that effect. It was
Lilith. She might have said, 'Armand Duval, where are my *marrons
glacé's*?' but all she said was, 'Hello.' After suavely introducing
Françoise to her as my mother and my mother as Françoise I
steered her to the rail.

'Won't Emu miss you?' I croaked offhandedly.

'He knows all about you,' she said, looking down into the bright
water. 'Don't worry. I told him that if he killed you I'd never speak
to him again.'

'Why did you let me?'

'I just liked your slouch hat. What do you call that thing in it
again?'

'A bash.'

'Anyway, by the time you get back, I'll be old.'

'Don't be silly,' I said, believing her. She turned around and looked up at the deck of the Harbour Bridge. I followed her gaze. She was looking at the blue cobweb. Then we did one of those quick, awkward kisses where each of you gets a nose in the eye.

Then she was gone, the crowd making a path for her as it always did. A siren went. They piped all visitors ashore. Drunks fell off the gangplanks. Could my loved ones tell from my eyes how much less I felt than they did? Catching my streamer as she stood with thousands of others at the rail of the dock, my mother was as brave as if she had never done this before. Which ship was it that she was seeing? Was it her husband or her son who stood at the other end of the swooping ribbon that grew straight, then taut, then snapped?

The lake of white light between the ship and the wharf grew wider. Behind the crowd on the roof of the dock I could just see Grogan jumping up and down. He appeared to have no clothes on at all. As the year turned, the tugs swung the ship's prow down harbour. From the stern I watched the lake of light divide into two pools, one of them going with me and the other staying. Passing between the Heads was like being born again.

17. THAT HE SHOULD LEAVE HIS HOUSE

The voyage was too tedious to be described in detail. Apart from the one occasion that I stepped over the border into Queensland, it was the first time I had ever been outside the confines of NSW. But the sense of adventure was nullified by the living conditions on the ship. Even a luxury liner is really just a bad play surrounded by water. It is a means of inducing hatred for your fellow men by trapping you in a confined space with too few of them to provide variety and too many to allow solitude. The *Bretagne* was all that and less. Every acceptable girl on the ship was being laid by a crew member before the ship was out of the Heads. This was a replacement crew who had all been flown out from the Persian Gulf. The previous crew had walked off the ship at Melbourne after one of the officers had shot an albatross.

With my two footballing companions I inhabited a phone-booth-sized cabinette on Deck Z, many feet below the waterline. One wall was curved. It was part of the propeller-shaft housing. If one of us wanted to get dressed the other two had to go back to bed. After we cleared the Barrier Reef we ran into a gale and spent a day heeled over at about twenty degrees from the vertical. One of the footballers chucked into the washbasin. The contents of his stomach, which had included two helpings of rhubarb crumble and custard, congealed in the basin. When the ship righted itself the surface of the solidified chunder remained at an angle, not to be removed until we docked in Singapore.

In Singapore we went by trishaw to Raffles, where I grandly ordered a round of lager for the three of us. The bill came to £47 – nearly all the money I had. What little cash was left over I spent on a taxi to Changi. The jail was full of Chinese pirates. They were guarded by Gurkhas. The Gurkha warrant officer showed me around. In this place the Japanese commandant had deliberately withheld supplies of rice polishings while the POWs wasted away from vitamin deficiency. In this place my father had weighed as much as I had when I was ten years old. I tried to imagine him having the dead flesh cleaned out of his ulcers with a heated teaspoon. I could not. It was all gone. He was gone. In Changi I realized that I would never find my father as he had been. It was no use looking. One day, in my imagination, he would return of his own accord.

On the way out of Singapore harbour the captain misunderstood the pilot. The ship went the wrong side of a buoy, hit a sandbar and turned towards the wharves. The anchors were dropped and the brakes were applied to the chains, but the ship's momentum was not easily checked. The links of the chains glowed cherry red. When they were hosed down the water was instantly transformed into geysers of steam. On the dock the stevedores in black shorts and flat conical hats looked up to see a 29,000-ton liner coming straight at them. They headed for the tall bamboo. The ship stopped just in time. A diver went down to check the damage. He surfaced to announce that one of the propeller shafts had a kink in it. Guess which one.

At reduced speed the ship limped across the Indian Ocean. The Greek entertainments officer entertained us by organizing Greek dancing displays, in which the prettier girl passengers showed us the skills they had learned from the crew during the day. The skills they had learned from the crew during the night we were left to imagine. Greek dancing consists of a man holding up a handkerchief, striking a masculine attitude and performing some extremely boring steps until a girl grabs hold of the other end of the handkerchief and performs some steps even more boring than his. Then a lot of other girls hold hands with each other and perform some steps which make everything you have previously seen look comparatively exciting. I would much rather have done lifeboat drill, but all the lifeboats had long ago been painted into position so that not even dynamite could possibly have released them. This was an additional factor to be considered when you tried to imagine – or rather tried not to imagine – the number of sharks who were following in our wake, passionate for leftover baklava.

For some reason the swimming pool, just when we needed it, was emptied, never to be filled again with anything except beer cans thrown into it by the circles of formation drinkers who sat cross-legged on the deck chanting, 'Who took the cookie from the cookie jar?' Then the ship stopped altogether. The temperature was roughly that of the surface of the sun, which didn't look very far away. Praying for release at the ship's rail, I watched a turtle go past on its way to the Red Sea. That was where we were supposed to be going, but we weren't. That night, as every other night, the film was *The Naked Jungle*, in which Charlton Heston and Eleanor Parker battle the killer ants of South America. The next day there was Greek dancing. The day after that, the ship moved.

Aden was a revelation. Until then my belief in God's indifference had been theoretical. In the Crater of Aden there were things on show that might have made Christ throw in the towel. Certainly there were wounds he would not have kissed. Beggars whose faces had been licked off by camels proffered children whose bones had been deliberately broken at birth. Catatonic with culture shock, the passengers of the good ship *Bretagne* bought transistor radios and binoculars. With the radios they could drown out the hum of flies and with the binoculars they could look somewhere else.

The Suez Canal still featured some wrecks from 1956. Lacking the cash to join an expedition to Cairo, I stayed on the ship as it crawled through to Port Said. Nasser's MiGs went by, up above the heat. I was down inside it. Port Said was like Coles or Woolworths, without the variety. Three products were on sale, all of them cranked out by a factory on the edge of town. They sold fake leather whips, fake leather wallets and fake leather television pouffes. The fake leather was made of compressed paper. The passengers of the *Bretagne* emptied the shops, which filled up again

just behind them. Nasser's police were omnipresent, making sure
nobody got hurt. Nobody was going to interfere with you as you
purchased the wherewithal for whipping yourself and counting
your money while watching television. You were safer than in St
Mary's Cathedral. The only danger was of being driven mad by
Nasser's charismatic gaze. His portrait was everywhere.

We missed out on Tangiers because of the pressing urgency to
keep a date with the dry dock in Southampton. But we did have
half a day in Athens. On the Acropolis I watched one of my compatriots carve his name into the Parthenon and heard another ask
where the camels were. The girl passengers raced into town to buy
hats with pom-poms and handkerchiefs for Greek dancing. But I
felt no less ignorant than my compatriots. The stone drapery on
the caryatids seemed to give off its own illumination, as if the
bright sun penetrated the surface before being reflected. It infuri-
ated me that I couldn't read the inscriptions. Their clear, clean look
only increased my suspicion that the real secrets of the tragedies
and the Platonic dialogues, which I had thought I knew something
about, lay in the sound of the language, and that until I could read
that I would know nothing. I was right about that, but confir-
mation lay far in the future. Now there was nothing to do except
return to Piraeus and commit myself into the hands of the sons of
Pericles for the last leg of the voyage. I don't suppose the lump of
rock outside the harbour would have looked any more significant
if I had known that its name was Salamis.

The *Bretagne* wasn't much of a ship. On her next voyage back
to Australia she hit the bottom of the harbour again, this time in
Piraeus. She caught fire and burned out. There was nothing left
but the hulk, which had to be blown up. But her job was done.
She had got me to England. In the Bay of Biscay on our last
afternoon at sea she ran before the gale, clumsily hurdling the
enormous swell. By midnight she was in the Channel. Undetected
from the bridge, I crouched out on deck in the prow, waiting to
see the lights of Southampton. They materialized about an hour
before dawn. They were just coloured lights and it was very cold.

I had never been so cold. White stuff was falling out of the sky. At
first I thought it was manna. The ship ground to a halt and waited
for morning. It shook gently on the vibration of the girl passengers
saying farewell to the crew. I went back down to Deck Z, lay on
my bunk and wondered what would happen next.

What happened next is another story. This story I had better
break off while I still have your patience, if I do. The longer I have
stayed in England, the more numerous and powerful my memories
of Sydney have grown. There is nothing like staying away for
bringing it with you. I have done my best to tell the truth about
what it was like, yet I am well aware that in the matter of my
own feelings I have not come near meeting my aim. My ideal of
autobiography has been set by Alfieri, whose description of a duel
he once fought in Hyde Park is mainly concerned with how he ran
backwards to safety. Perhaps because I am not even yet sufficiently
at peace with myself, I have not been able to meet those standards
of honesty. Nothing I have said is factual except the bits that sound
like fiction.

By the time this book is published I will be forty years old.
When I left Sydney I boasted that I would be gone for five years. I
was to be gone three times that and more. During that time most
of those who came away have gone back. Before Gough Whitlam
came to power, having to return felt like defeat. Afterwards it felt
like the natural thing to do. Suddenly Australia began offering its
artists all the recognition they had previously been denied. It took
a kind of perversity to refuse the lure. Perhaps I did the wrong
thing. Eventually fear plays a part: when you are too long gone, to
return even for a month feels like time travel. So you try to forget.
But the memories keep on coming. I have tried to keep them under
control. I hope I have not overdone it, and killed the flavour.
Because Sydney is so real in my recollection that I can taste it.

It tastes like happiness. I have never ceased to feel orphaned,
but nor have I ever felt less than lucky – a lucky member of a lucky
generation. In this century of all centuries we have been allowed to
grow up and grow old in peace. There is a Buster Keaton film in

which he is standing around innocently when the facade of a house falls on him. An open window in the facade passes over his body, so that he is left untouched.

I can see the Fun Doctor juggling for us at Kogarah Infants' School. One of the balls hits the floor with a thud. Then what looks like the same ball lands on his head. I can hear the squeak that the mica window panels of the Kosi stove made when I scorched them with the red-hot poker. When Jeanette Elphick came back on a visit from Hollywood they drove her around town in a blue Customline with her new name painted in huge yellow letters along the side: VICTORIA SHAW. On Empire Night when we threw pieces of fibro into the bonfire they cracked like rifle shots. Every evening for weeks before Empire Night I used to lay my fireworks out on the lounge-room carpet, which became impregnated with the smell of gunpowder. Peter Moulton kept his fireworks in a Weetabix carton. On the night, a spark from the fire drifted into the carton and the whole lot went up. A rocket chased Gail Thorpe, who was only just back from therapy. She must have thought it was all part of the treatment.

At the Legacy Party in Clifton Gardens I got a No. 4 Meccano set. On hot nights before the nor'easter came you changed into your cossie and ran under the sprinkler. At Sans Souci baths I dive-bombed a jelly blubber for a dare. If you rubbed sand into the sting it hurt less. Bindies in the front lawn made you limp to the steps of the porch and bend over to pick them out. Sandfly bites needed Calamine lotion that dried to a milky crust. From Rose Bay at night you could hear the lions making love in Taronga Park. If the shark bell rang and you missed the wave, you were left out there alone beyond the third line of breakers. Every shadow had teeth. Treading water in frantic silence, you felt afraid enough to run Christ-like for the shore.

At the Harvest Festivals in church the area behind the pulpit was piled high with tins of IXL fruit for the old-age pensioners. We had collected the tinned fruit from door to door. Most of it came from old-age pensioners. Some of them must have got their own stuff back. Others were less lucky. Hunting for cicadas in the peppercorns and the willows, you were always in search of the legendary black prince, but invariably he turned out to be a redeye. The ordinary cicada was called a pisser because he squirted mud at you. The most beautiful cicada was the yellow Monday. He was as yellow as a canary and transparent as crystal. When he lifted his wings in the sunlight the membranes were like the deltas of little rivers. The sun shone straight through him. It shone straight through all of us.

It shone straight through everything, and I suppose it still does. As I begin this last paragraph, outside my window a misty afternoon drizzle gently but inexorably soaks the City of London. Down there in the street I can see umbrellas commiserating with each other. In Sydney Harbour, twelve thousand miles away and ten hours from now, the yachts will be racing on the crushed diamond water under a sky the texture of powdered sapphires. It would be churlish not to concede that the same abundance of natural blessings which gave us the energy to leave has every right to call us back. All in, the whippy's taken. Pulsing like a beacon through the days and nights, the birthplace of the fortunate sends out its invisible waves of recollection. It always has and it always will, until even the last of us come home.

FALLING TOWARDS ENGLAND

To Chester and John Cummings

I had already noticed with various people that the affectation of praiseworthy sentiments is not the only way of covering up reprehensible ones, but that a more up-to-date method is to put these latter on exhibition, so that one has the air of at least being forthright.

Proust, *Le Temps retrouvé*

All censure of a man's self is oblique praise. It is in order to show how much he can spare.

Johnson

Contents